PERFECTIONISM

What's Bad About Being Too Good

PERFECTIONISM

What's Bad About Being Too Good

Miriam Adderholdt-Elliott, Ph.D.

Edited by Pamela Espeland
Illustrated by Caroline Price

*Free
Spirit*
PUBLISHING

Library of Congress Cataloging-in-Publication Data

Adderholdt-Elliott, Miriam, 1957-
  Perfectionism: what's bad about being too good.

  Bibliography: p.
  Includes index.
  Summary: Discusses the dangers of being a perfectionist, with tips for easing up on oneself, gaining control
over life, and getting professional help.
    1. Perfectionism (Personality trait)—Juvenile
literature. 2. Ambition—Juvenile literature. 3. Mental
health—Juvenile literature. [1. Perfectionism
(Personality trait)] I. Espeland, Pamela, 1951-
II. Price, Caroline, ill. III. Title.

BF698.35.P47A23   1987   158'.1   86-81130
ISBN 0-915793-07-5 (pbk.)

Printed in the United States of America

10   9   8   7   6   5   4   3

Cover and text design: MacLean & Tuminelly

FREE SPIRIT PUBLISHING
123 N. Third St., Suite 716
Minneapolis, MN 55401
(612) 338-2068

DEDICATION

To the memory of my father, the Rev. C.C. Adderholdt.
His love of learning and quest for knowledge
were instilled within me at an early age.

CONTENTS

ACKNOWLEDGMENTS

I want to thank Dr. Mary Frasier of the University of Georgia for her immense help while directing my doctoral dissertation. Her expertise in the fields of gifted education, counseling, and bibliotherapy were invaluable to both my dissertation and this book. Her kindness, concern, and long hours were greatly appreciated.

Thanks to Judy Galbraith, whose first and foremost concern in publishing is the welfare of gifted children. She is extremely talented and we in gifted education benefit from her dedication.

Thanks to my editor, Pamela Espeland, whose sense of humor and creativity were extremely valuable.

To my family for their continued support in my education and career, I give many thanks. And to my husband, Bryan Elliott, I am especially grateful. His emotional support, love, and concern supported me throughout this project. He has helped me try to find balance in my life.

FOREWORD

Various things can trigger the anxiety and stress that accompany perfectionism — for example, being asked to write this foreword.

I had to do it right! I couldn't let Miriam down by writing anything less than a perfect foreword. After all, she was my first doctoral student. I went to the library and read the forewords in several books. I even considered doing an ERIC search. I wrote and rewrote the first sentence, tore up what I wrote and paced the floor. I berated myself for making such a simple thing so difficult. As each day passed, I told myself, "It's only a foreword; I'll set aside an hour tomorrow and get it done." Then that hour came, and I froze. I cleaned my desk. I answered letters. I did other pressing tasks. Meanwhile, the foreword turned into THE FOREWORD and loomed large in my mind.

My personal experience as a perfectionist, and my professional experience with gifted young people, demonstrate the need for this book. It represents the first comprehensive coverage of a very important topic in the education of gifted individuals. It provides a much needed discussion of the psychological constructs that underlie perfectionism. It is not only the logic of this book that will be useful, but the opportunity it provides to recognize, examine, accept, and understand better the phenomenon of perfectionism.

A review of the literature on giftedness reveals that little attention has been paid to this subject. Yet it is one of the most critical issues a gifted young person faces. More than any other group, the gifted suffer the most because of their tendencies toward perfectionism — sometimes for all the "right" reasons. Because they are capable of excelling far beyond the average, they are pushed by everyone to strive and excel. But often the biggest push comes from inside themselves.

This book is long overdue. I welcome it.

Mary Mack Frasier, Ph.D.
Associate Professor, The University of Georgia at Athens
President, National Association for Gifted Children
Perfectionist

HOW MUCH OF A PERFECTIONIST ARE YOU?

Have you ever caught yourself thinking or feeling "I have to please everyone" . . . "I always have to finish what I start" . . . "I mustn't disappoint anyone" . . . "I want everyone to like me" . . . "I have to do everything well, not just the things I know I'm good at" . . . . ??? If any of these sound familiar to you, there's a good chance you have perfectionist tendencies.

How much of a perfectionist are you? This exercise can help you find out. Read each statement, then rate each one according to whether you *strongly agree* (+ 2), *agree somewhat* (+ 1), *can't decide* (0), *disagree somewhat* (-1), or *strongly disagree* (-2).* Answer with your *first* thought to get the truest response.

———— 1. I'm critical of people who don't live up to my expectations.
———— 2. I get upset if I don't finish something I start.
———— 3. I do things precisely down to the very last detail.

* Adapted from "Some people are perfect . . . Or try to be!," *Current Health II* volume 4 (January 1978), pp. 17-19. Permission granted by the publisher, General Learning Corporation.

_____ 4. I argue about test scores I don't agree with, even when they won't affect my final grade.
_____ 5. After I finish something I often feel dissatisfied.
_____ 6. I feel guilty when I don't achieve something I set out to do.
_____ 7. When a teacher hands back one of my papers, I look for mistakes before looking for right answers or positive comments.
_____ 8. I compare my test scores with those of other good students in my class.
_____ 9. It's hard for me to laugh at my own mistakes.
_____ 10. If I don't like the way I've done something, I start over and keep at it until I get it right.

Now add up your ratings to learn where you fall on the Perfectionism Continuum.

If your total is between + 15 and + 20, you're Too Good To Be True.

Maybe you're exaggerating your own capabilities and skills. And maybe you're used to exaggerating them because people have always expected you to be perfect.

If your total is between + 10 and + 14, you're Too Good For Your Own Good.

You're trying too hard — and it's time to ask yourself why.

If your total is between + 5 and + 9, you're a Borderline Perfectionist.

Certain events in your life may push you over the line into Full-Fledged Perfectionism, but you usually manage to roll with the punches without going to extremes.

If your total is between + 1 and + 4, you're a Healthy Pursuer of Excellence.

You enjoy doing well, but you can turn your pursuit of excellence on and off at will (in other words, *you* drive *it,* not the other way around). You probably spread your talents and abilities into several areas of life: academics, friendships, your health and appearance, hobbies, and play.

If your total is between 0 and -5, you're Used to Hanging Loose.

Maybe you've made a conscious effort to be less perfectionist, or maybe you were born knowing how to relax and take it easy.

If your total is between -6 and -10, you're A Little TOO Relaxed.

Your favorite song is "Que Sera, Sera" ("What Will Be, Will Be") and your favorite activity is lying in a hammock feeling the earth turn . . . A slight exaggeration, perhaps, but there is such a thing as overdoing *under*doing!

If your total is between -11 and -20, you're Barely Breathing.

And maybe you're exaggerating your own coolness. Read through the statements again, and this time respond to them honestly. You can't be apathetic about *everything!*

Did this exercise teach you something you didn't already know? Probably not; most perfectionists are aware of who and what they are. But one thing you may not know is that you're *not* alone. Dr. David Burns of the University of Pennsylvania estimates that about half the population of the United States has perfectionist tendencies.

For most people, perfectionism isn't a big problem. It can be, however, for one group in particular: gifted kids. In *The Gifted Kids Survival Guide (For Ages 11-18)*, perfectionism is listed as one of the Eight Great Gripes of Gifted Kids. Students told author Judy Galbraith, "Parents (teachers, friends) expect us to be perfect, to 'do our best' *all* the time!"

Why are gifted kids so prone to perfectionism, and why is it a particular gripe for them? Here's one possible answer:

■ Many have a long history of "A's" and "A + 's" in school, and often they carry the desire for perfectionism into other areas of their lives.

Here's another:

■ Many are so used to success that when they do less than the best, they feel like failures. It hurts so much that they decide never to let it happen again.

What's bad about being too good? For some people, plenty.

In June of 1986, runner 21-year-old Kathy Ormsby ran her last race. Less than two months earlier the North Carolina State junior had broken the women's intercollegiate record for the 10,000-meter run. In June she competed in the NCAA Outdoor Track and Field championships in Indianapolis. With 3,500 meters left to go, she veered off the track and kept running — out of the Indiana University Stadium, into the night, to a nearby bridge, and off. She fell 40 feet onto a flood plain and damaged her spine so severely that she is now paralyzed from the waist down. She told her coach that she had jumped intentionally.

Kathy Ormsby was a gifted athlete and a straight-A student who always wore a smile. She was so outstanding in every way that her hometown had named a day in her honor. Why did she do it? Her father said that she had always been an overachiever and a perfectionist. She put so much pressure on herself that her teammates called her the "pusher." Whenever she failed to come in first, she felt as if she was letting everyone down — including herself.

Maybe you haven't ever thought about jumping off a bridge. But maybe you *have* felt like screaming over the pressure you feel from inside and outside, or closing the door to your room and staying there forever, or telling your parents and teachers and friends to JUST LEAVE YOU ALONE. Perfectionism can be a heavy burden because, let's face it, NOBODY'S perfect — not even the gifted student who excels at almost everything he or she tries to do.

This book is about the impossibility of perfection. It's about knowing the difference between doing your best and overdoing it, and about striking a balance between the three main areas of life: work and school, play and hobbies, and family and social relationships. It shows you why it's important to give yourself a break every now and then, to be pleased with who and what you are here and now, and to enjoy the healthy pursuit of excellence.

What's the difference between perfectionism and the pursuit of excellence? Read these and see:

The pursuit of excellence = doing the research necessary for a term paper, working hard on it, turning it in on time, and feeling good about it.

Perfectionism = doing three drafts, staying up two nights in a row, and handing your paper in late *because you had to get it right* — and still feeling bad about it.

The pursuit of excellence = studying for a test ahead of time, taking it with confidence, and feeling good about your score of 96.

Perfectionism = studying at the last minute (after three days of chronic procrastination), taking the test with sweaty palms, and feeling depressed about your 96 because your best friend got a 98.

The pursuit of excellence = choosing to work on group projects because you enjoy learning from the varied experiences and approaches of different people.

Perfectionism = always working alone because NO ONE can do as good a job as you and you're not about to let anyone else slide by on YOUR A.

The pursuit of excellence = accepting an award with pride even though the engraver misspelled your name. (You know that it can be fixed later at the jewelry store.)

Perfectionism = accepting the award resentfully because that dumb engraver didn't get your name right.

The pursuit of excellence = reading the story you wrote for the school paper and noticing that the editor made some changes to the copy that really improved it.

Perfectionism = throwing a near tantrum because the editor dared to tamper with your work.

The pursuit of excellence = going out with people who are interesting, likeable, and fun to be with.

Perfectionism = refusing to go out with people who aren't straight-A students.

The pursuit of excellence = being willing to try new things, take risks, and learn from your experiences *and* your mistakes.

Perfectionism = avoiding new experiences because you're terrified of making mistakes.

In my work as a teacher and while doing research with young gifted women, I've spoken at length with a number of devoted perfectionists. Like Ann, who used to drop courses rather than risk getting a B — and then have to go to summer school to make up the courses she dropped. And Jennifer, who stuffed her locker with term papers she refused to turn in because "they weren't good enough" — and ended up getting C's for not handing in her work. I also have perfectionist tendencies of my own, so I know how hard it is to resist them!

This book comes out of my experience, my studies, and the proof I have seen that you *can* put the lid on perfectionism. And you don't have to sacrifice any of your will to succeed, your push to achieve, or your desire to be the best you can be.

Hard to believe? Then read what three reformed perfectionists have to say:

*"It was when I stopped trying to do everything **right** that I started doing things **well**."*

Janet, 15

"Suddenly I had time and energy left over for other things that were important to me."

Max, 13

"It's great not to have to be the perfect student, perfect daughter, perfect sister, and perfect friend. I can just be myself — and people like me anyway."

Talia, 16

Conquering your perfectionism may release other abilities you didn't know you had. And it will certainly make your life easier, more relaxed, more satisfying — and a *lot* more fun.

Miriam Adderholdt-Elliott
Hickory, North Carolina

CHAPTER 1

WHY PEOPLE BECOME PERFECTIONISTS

Perfectionism isn't a disease; you didn't catch it. Perfectionism isn't hereditary; you weren't born with it. So how did you end up being a perfectionist?

Some experts believe that perfectionism is a result of social learning that occurs during childhood. Family pressure, self-pressure, social pressure, media pressure, and unrealistic role models combine in a Big Push that propels you into a lifetime of worrying, feeling guilty, and working too hard.

Families often reward "eager beaver" behavior — especially in a first-born child. There may be several reasons for this. For one, first-time parents are usually insecure. If their young son or daughter turns out to be a real go-getter, they're likely to think, "Hey, we must be doing a great job as parents!" Then they go on to encourage and reinforce fast-track learning.

In addition, firstborn children spend more time around adults than those who come later in the birth order. They learn adult vocabulary, model adult behaviors, and measure themselves according to adult standards of achievement. Adults may reinforce this by expecting them to live up to those standards.

Not surprisingly, firstborns are identified as gifted and talented more often than any-other-borns; they tend to be great organizers and may be very achievement-oriented. But, according to Kevin Leman, Ph.D., author of *The Birth Order Book: Why You Are the Way You Are,* they are also seen for counseling more often than any-other-borns. One reason may be their propensity for perfectionism.

Firstborns have hardly cornered the market on perfectionism, however. There are plenty of second- and thirdborns who show all the signs. That's because there are numerous other reasons why some kids develop these traits — another common one being the presence of perfectionist parents. (In a way, perfectionism *is* hereditary, because it seems to pass from one generation to the next.)

The Superkid Syndrome

The Superkid Syndrome is a fairly recent development. For some, it starts very early — even in the womb. Parents eager for their offspring to be smart and successful begin reading and talking to a child long before it's born. Then, when the baby does come into the world, the parents keep up their efforts to make sure that their son or daughter gets ahead and stays there. One way to do this is by piling on the programs and activities: baby gymnastics, baby aerobics, baby swimming, Suzuki music lessons for tots, French for toddlers, flashcards, early reading, early math, and so on.

Educational psychologists call this "hothousing" preschoolers. Just as a florist gets flowering plants to bloom sooner by raising them in a green-house, parents try to give their kids' development a boost by providing them with extra stimulation and opportunities for learning skills in advance of their age peers. It's an approach that has generated a lot of controversy. On the one side are those who feel that kids can and should learn more and sooner; on the other are those who believe that childhood is already too short. Plus the more time a child spends on structured activities, the less time there is for the unstructured free play that gives rise to creative thinking.

The school-age Superkid often continues to be superscheduled — with piano lessons, ballet classes, baton instruction, gymnastics, softball, ice-skating practice, swimming, scouts, hockey practice, special courses in art and music appreciation, organized play groups, and on and on and on . . . . *In moderation,* these are all excellent activities. But together they can result in circuit overload.

Many authorities in childhood education are speaking out against the Superkid Syndrome:

- Dr. Benjamin Spock voices strong objections to fast-track schooling and forcing kids into the fast lane. He believes that our society is much too concerned with competition and materialism and should focus instead on other values — like cooperation and kindness.

- Robert Keesham (you know him as Captain Kangaroo) has been lecturing on the stresses placed on toddlers who are taught too much too soon. He talks about the importance of setting aside time for simple, non-brain-draining activities, such as taking walks and observing nature.

Child psychologist David Elkind has found that higher-income families are more likely than lower-income families to pressure their kids. There's extra emphasis on wearing the "right" brand-name clothes, taking the "right" lessons, participating in the "right" organized activities, and going to the "right" private preschools.

"Hothoused" toddlers and Superkids are fairly recent phenomena. Before the middle of the twentieth century, hardly anyone thought of pushing children to achieve before they started school. Then came Head Start, Sesame Street, and the Better Baby Institute.

- **Head Start** was a program conducted by the United States government during the 1950s and 1960s for the benefit of children from low-income families who received little at-home intellectual stimulation. The goal was to provide them with preschool training so they wouldn't be so far behind other kids when they started primary school.

- **Sesame Street,** which first went on the air in 1968, uses television to teach counting, vocabulary, and the alphabet to preschoolers. Like Head Start, it was intended primarily for low-income, inner-city kids, but it caught on quickly at all levels of society.

- The **Better Baby Institute** was founded in 1977 by Dr. Glenn Doman. More than 20 years earlier, he had founded the Institutes for the Achievement of Human Potential to treat brain-injured children by teaching them with special flashcards. The Better Baby Institute uses similar techniques and methods to teach non-handicapped babies reading, math, and a variety of other subjects from art history to zoology — even foreign languages.

Today many psychologists are saying that instead of pressuring little kids to learn facts and read flashcards, it's better to take them on nature walks, build sandcastles with them, and spend time together playing imaginative games and participating in unstructured activities. There's also some question as to whether children who start school knowing more than their age peers actually stay ahead in the years to come.

In other words, the Superkid may not be that advanced after all. And the price for pushing a child to achieve may not be worth it. Too much stress may even *block* learning.

The Workaholic Kid

We've heard of workaholic adults — but workaholic *kids?* According to psychologist Erik Erikson, children between ages 6 and 12 are at risk for becoming workaholics if they are rewarded for the things they *do* rather than for the personal qualities they have and are developing. In other words, the child who is praised for bringing home perfect papers but not for being a nice person, having a sense of humor, being playful, taking risks, showing kindness and gentleness, and being a good friend is likely to think that work is the most important part of life. The child gets "hooked" on working hard because he or she knows that it will bring rewards.

Working can be as addictive as drugs or gambling. Unlike drugs or gambling, however, it's something that parents support and encourage without realizing the danger. The parents who brag that Alvin spends four hours a day on his homework probably aren't aware that Alvin may need to spend some of that time just having fun. But if the parents keep rewarding Alvin for sitting at his desk, that's what he'll keep doing.

The problem of adult workaholism has received a lot of attention in recent years. Studies have shown that workaholics suffer from higher stress levels and have a greater tendency to "burn out" than people whose lives are more balanced. Some adult workaholics literally don't know how to relax; they work day in and day out without ever taking a vacation. It's hardly a healthy lifestyle!

It's important to work, but it's also important to play. It's good to study, but it's also good to goof off on occasion. Straight A's are commendable, but so is an active social life.

How balanced is *your* life? What would you change if you could? (And how soon can you start?)

> "In order that people may be happy in their work, these three things are needed: They must be fit for it. They must not do too much of it. And they must have a sense of success in it."
>
> *John Ruskin*

The Message of the Media

The next time you watch TV, pay attention to how many times the word "perfect" is used as part of a sales pitch. You'll see ads for "perfect" cars, ice cream, soap, vacations, jeans, nail polish, dog food — you name it. But cars break down, some soaps make us itch, vacations can be plagued by sunburn and mosquitoes . . . you get the idea. Regardless of what copywriters claim, *nothing* is perfect!

Now consider how that word is used to describe the way we should live and the kinds of relationships we should strive for. We've all heard of the "perfect romance," the "perfect marriage," and the "perfect family." But some romances fizzle, many marriages end in divorce, and the typical family has plenty of arguments and off days.

TV, magazines, and the movies lead us to believe that everyone should be thin, gorgeous, rich, and successful. Dads should have all the answers; moms should be able to work all day and come home to fix dinner for their families, *and* take care of the house, *and* help the kids with their homework. We're told that it's possible to have perfect houses and perfect jobs, perfect complexions and perfect bodies. We *know* that's not how things really are, but we *wish* they could be that way — and we sometimes convince our-selves that we can *make* them that way if we try hard enough.

It's tough to resist the pressures to be perfect that we get from our families, our culture, and the media. It's tough not to compound these by setting unrealistic goals for ourselves and pushing ourselves to achieve more and faster. It's tough to let go of the belief that we can do anything we set out to do. After all, we're bright and we're capable — what's to stop us?

There's nothing wrong with wanting to do our best, but there is a dark side to perfectionism. It messes with our minds, and it messes up our bodies. Let's find out how and why.

If you want to read more about some of the ideas in this chapter, try:

The Birth Order Book — Why You Are the Way You Are by Kevin Leman, Ph.D. (Old Tappan, New Jersey: Fleming H. Revell Company, 1985)

The Hurried Child — Growing Up Too Fast Too Soon by David Elkind, Ph.D. (Reading, Massachusetts: Addison-Wesley Publishing Company, 1981)

All Grown Up and No Place to Go — Teenagers in Crisis by David Elkind, Ph.D. (Reading, Massachusetts: Addison-Wesley Publishing Company, 1984)

Workaholics — Living With Them, Working With Them by Marilyn Machlowitz (New York: New American Library, 1981)

Whiz Kids — Success at an Early Age by Marilyn Machlowitz (New York: Arbor House Publishing Company, 1985)

CHAPTER 2

WHAT PERFECTIONISM DOES TO YOUR MIND

In 1984, when a group of University of Georgia women students were tested to determine the relationship between perfectionism and self-concept, a fascinating pattern emerged: The higher the perfectionism score, the lower the self-concept score. The young women were tying their identities to their performance.

You've heard people say things like, "There's Jennifer. She's a straight-A student." The trouble is, Jennifer has heard it, too, and that's how she perceives and defines herself. What happens if she gets a B? Her self-concept is shaken. She feels that she is not "herself." It doesn't matter that she still looks the same, has the same values, likes the same foods, and wears the same holey sneakers; she feels *different*.

FIVE FAMOUS PEOPLE WHO DIDN'T GET STRAIGHT A'S

Charles Darwin

He did poorly in the early grades and failed a university medical course.

Albert Einstein

He performed badly in almost all of his high-school courses and failed his college entrance exams.

Sir Winston Churchill

He was at the bottom of his class in one school and twice failed the entrance exams to another.

Pablo Picasso

He could barely read and write when his father pulled him out of school at age 10. A tutor hired to prepare him for secondary school gave up and quit.

Paul Ehrlich

This 1908 Nobel Prize-winner in medicine did badly in school, hated exams, and couldn't write compositions or give oral presentations.

If you're searching for something to tie your identity to, a straight-A average is a poor choice. It's simply too vulnerable and hard to maintain. (One B and it's all over!) I've known a number of straight-A high-school students who have determined to keep it up once they hit college, ignoring the fact that the competition has suddenly gotten much tougher. High schools have to let *everybody* in, but colleges get to choose their populations from among hundreds and sometimes thousands of applicants.

One young man found out what this meant during the first assembly at his college. He had been a star performer all during high school — straight A's, National Merit finalist, sky-high SAT scores, and class valedictorian. He learned that day that nearly half of the members of his freshman class had been valedictorians, too. Suddenly he was no big deal, and it was a blow to his sense of himself.

There are other signs of achievement to which perfectionists link their identities: medals, ribbons, trophies, setting records, always getting the lead in the school play, being elected student body president — and even being identified as gifted.

A perfectionist whose identity is at stake will go to desperate lengths to try to save it. Some students lose sleep and make themselves sick trying to maintain their straight-A selves. Some cheat. Some tune out and drop out rather than face what they perceive as "failure." Some turn to alcohol or drugs.

Going to the game tonight?

I can't. I grounded myself for getting a B on a test. I have to do better than that.

Games Perfectionists Play

When you start believing that achievement and self-worth are one and the same, your thinking becomes convoluted. Perfectionists use a number of tricks and stratagems — often unconsciously — to protect the picture they have of themselves. See if any of these sound familiar:

■ Mood Swinging

You set a goal for yourself (for example: to ace a math test). You do it — and you feel great!

But you *don't* ace the next one — and you feel AWFUL. You develop a serious case of the blues. Your friends and family notice and try to reassure you with praise, but you're prickly and irritable and suspicious of their motives. Why would they praise you? You're not worth it; you didn't get that A you were after!

Then along comes the next math test, and you ace it, and you're back to feeling great again.

It's exhausting!

> "The battle to keep up appearances unnecessarily, the mask — whatever name you give creeping perfectionism — robs us of our energies."
>
> *Robin Worthington*

■ The Numbers Game

The *quantity* of achievements or actions becomes more important than the *quality*. The emphasis is on how many trophies you win, papers you write, awards you receive, honors you reap — not what they're for or what they're worth. No number is ever high enough; you just keep counting.

■ Telescopic Thinking

You use both ends of a telescope when viewing your achievements. When looking at the goals you haven't met, you use the magnifying end so they appear much larger than they really are. But when looking at those you have met, you use the "minifying" end so they appear minute and insignificant.

You win the district tennis match, but you can't feel good about it because you haven't yet won the state. Or you win the state, and you pass it off because it isn't Wimbledon.

■ Focusing on the Future

You give an especially brilliant speech during the debate. Everybody comes up afterward and tells you that you were positively inspiring. But you're thinking of all the things you forgot to say. Or your mind is already on next week's essay contest — what if you don't outdo yourself in that, too?

Don't even try to sit back and savor your success; that's not what perfectionists do. There's no time — not when you're already planning the future, and the things you MUST do to succeed then.

■ Pining Over the Past

"If only I had done this . . . " "Why didn't I do that . . . " "This wouldn't have happened if I had started sooner . . . " "If I had put down that answer instead, I would have gotten an A instead of a B . . . . " Thoughts like these keep you stuck in the same old groove of the same old record.

■ Putting Your Goals First

Given a choice between sleeping and studying, you study — even if it means drinking gallons of coffee, taking No-Doz, pinching yourself to stay awake, and making yourself sick. Or given the choice between going to a movie and working some more on a school project, you stay home. Your goals come first over fun or friends or your own good health.

■ Getting It Right

You're not satisfied with anything but perfection, so you do the same thing again . . . and again . . . and again until you get it right. Maybe you repeat the same course in school until you get the A you're determined to have. Or you play the same piece of music over and over and over and over and over and over and over and over and over and over.

■ All-Or-Nothing Thinking

You're not satisfied unless you have it all — all A's, all the track trophies, all the academic awards your school can give, all the leads in all the plays. One B or one second place is enough to tip you over into feeling that you've failed, that you're not good enough.

Sometimes parents encourage this attitude. When Lisa started seventh grade, her parents said, "We'll give you ten dollars for each A on your report card — as long as you get all A's. If you get even one B, we won't give you anything." Lisa learned something besides all-or-nothing thinking. She learned that her parents' love and approval depended on her performance.

A PERFECTIONIST MYTH: THE FALL OF ICARUS

The master craftsman Daedalus and his young son, Icarus, were prisoners of King Minos of Crete. The King also had a son, but it was a terrible beast, half-man and half-bull, called the Minotaur. Minos instructed Daedalus to build a labyrinth to house the Minotaur. Daedalus did as he was told, only to learn that he and Icarus would be imprisoned in the Labyrinth for the rest of their lives.

Daedalus thought of a way to escape. For years he collected the feathers that fell from the birds who flew over the Labyrinth. Then he fashioned frames from wood and attached the feathers to the frames with wax and twine. He made a pair of wings for himself, and another for his son. As he was helping Icarus strap on his wings, Daedalus warned him to keep a middle course over the sea — not to fly too close to the sun, or too near the sea.

The two sailed out into the air, over the sea toward freedom. Icarus had never felt such exhilaration. His great wings carried him effortlessly over the waves. He flew higher and higher still, closer and closer to the sun, disregarding his father's warning. Why not go five feet more, then ten feet, then twenty?

Daedalus shouted commands at him, but Icarus ignored those, too. Then it happened: the wax melted, Icarus's wings came apart, and he fell like a stone into the sea.

The Procrastination Trap

How could a perfectionist also be a procrastinator? It sounds impossible, but in fact it's quite common. Studies have shown that perfectionism and procrastination often go hand in hand.

For the perfectionist, procrastination acts as an insurance policy. Remember that the perfectionist has to get everything right, and any performance short of spectacular is a "failure." Naturally this piles on the pressure. To relieve it somewhat, and to delay the possibility that a performance might not be perfect, the perfectionist puts things off.

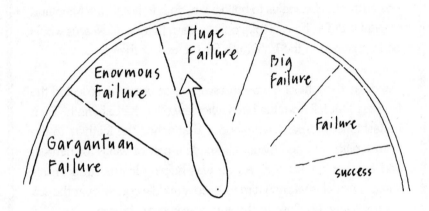

And then the inevitable happens: the panic buzzer sounds! The test is tomorrow morning . . . or the paper is due on Monday and it's already Thursday night . . . . Now the perfectionist goes into overdrive, pulling all-nighters and working furiously to get the job done. Needless to say, quality suffers. But in the perfectionist's mind, that's okay — because *how can you possibly do a perfect job if you simply don't have enough time?*

For the perfectionist, starting a new project is almost always a turn-off because each new beginning is a step on the road to possible failure.

Sue was in her first year of college when her procrastination habit caught up with her. As usual, she waited until the last minute before studying for a final. Knowing that she'd be up all night, she decided to go to a classroom on campus so she wouldn't keep her roommate awake. Her college was a small private school for women, so she simply threw on a coat over her nightgown and headed out. She got to the classroom, studied most of the night, and just before dawn decided to take a short nap on a table. The table was so hard that she thought she'd only be able to sleep a few minutes.

Several hours later, she awoke to find the class staring down at her!

This story has its funny side, but there are others that aren't funny at all. Of perfectionists who are refused admission to colleges because they couldn't get their applications in on time. Of people who lose their jobs because they can't let go of one project and move on to the next. Of kids who get so far behind in their schoolwork that they finally give up and drop out.

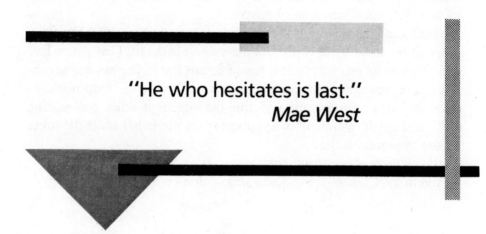

"He who hesitates is last."
Mae West

Procrastination is a complex problem that leads to irrational behaviors. Perfectionists often resort to one (or more) of the following to help hide their fear of being "imperfect":

■ **Not starting a project.**

"If I don't start something," perfectionists think, "I can't fail." So they write letters, catch up on their reading, clean out their desk . . . anything to keep busy and avoid the work that really needs doing.

■ **Not handing in a finished project.**

"It's done," perfectionists think, "but it's not good enough!" Often, procrastinating students ask for incomplete grades rather than risk getting less than an A.

■ **Starting so many projects that there isn't time to complete any one of them.**

"If only I didn't have so much to do," perfectionists think, "I could get something done!" Projects, assignments, and papers pile up until there's no way to finish any of them, much less all of them.

Jane Burka, Ph.D. and Lenora Yuen, Ph.D. have a counseling service in California especially for procrastinators. They hold workshops in which students learn to break their old self-defeating behavior patterns, set more realistic goals for themselves, reapportion their time, divide large tasks into more manageable parts, and reward themselves for each accomplishment, regardless of how small it seems.

Burka and Yuen have written a book, *Procrastination: Why You Do It, What To Do About It* that deals with this subject in detail. They define five main reasons for procrastination: fear of failure, fear of success, fear of control, fear of separation, and fear of attachment. Their "cure" for procrastination includes a combination of time-management skills, goal-setting skills, and the development of a support system to help handle the stress caused by procrastination.

If you're caught in the procrastination trap, here are ten "escape tips" for you to try. Choose one and get going — don't put it off!

Ten Tips For Procrastinators

1. Allow more time than you think a project will take. For example, if you think that writing an essay will take two hours, give yourself three or even four hours to do it.

2. Set realistic goals, but don't set them in stone. Stay flexible.

3. Break down big and intimidating projects into smaller, more doable ones.

4. Reward yourself after each accomplishment, large or small.

5. Make a conscious effort to realize that your paper, project, or whatever can't be perfect. Getting a grasp on this fact helps deflate the fear of failure.

6. Develop a "backwards schedule." Start with the things you most enjoy doing — the things you usually save for last and don't get around to at all. *Then* add the things you're supposed to do. Plan to have fun without feeling guilty.

7. Begin your day with your most difficult task, or the one you enjoy least. The rest of the day will seem easy by comparison.

8. Keep a diary of your progress — the things you accomplish each day. Read it over from time to time and feel proud of what you've done.

9. Remove distractions from your workplace. Keep food, TV, magazines, games, and other temptations out of your way.

10. Keep a list of backup projects — things you mean to do when you have time. Once you've made tips 1-9 part of your life, you *will* have the time to do them; use it productively!

Writer's Block, Test Anxiety, and Other Problems for Perfectionists

Can't put pen to paper? Too timid to touch the typewriter? Maybe you're afraid that what you're about to write won't be up to your own too-high standards. Writer's block is a common complaint for perfectionists.

Sweaty palms and a speedy heartbeat on the morning of the test? No wonder you're anxious; there's a chance you might not get every answer right!

Has your get up and go got up and went? Even the most hardworking perfectionist can become frustrated after years of attempting the impossible. Questions like "What's the use?" and "Why should I even try?" start making sense. The end result, oddly enough, is laziness. The dynamics behind it are more complex than simple sloth, but the end result is the same: the perfectionist lies around and does little or nothing.

Do you suffer frequent bouts with the blues? Times when it doesn't seem worth it to climb out of bed? Headaches, listlessness, crying jags? These are all signs of depression — another perfectionist specialty.

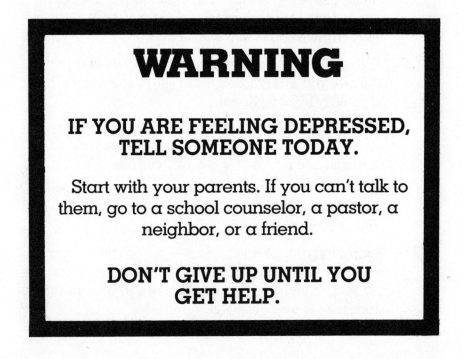

WARNING

IF YOU ARE FEELING DEPRESSED, TELL SOMEONE TODAY.

Start with your parents. If you can't talk to them, go to a school counselor, a pastor, a neighbor, or a friend.

DON'T GIVE UP UNTIL YOU GET HELP.

The Paralyzed Perfectionist

When you're unsure or afraid of where you're going, the safest bet is to go nowhere. When you don't want to risk being wrong, the surest thing to do is nothing. A lot of perfectionists take refuge in inertia — defined as a state of total rest. They become mentally and emotionally paralyzed.

If you could read the mind of a paralyzed perfectionist, here are some of the rationalizations you might see:

"If I never complete that project, I don't have to risk getting a bad grade"

"If I never write that short story/paint that picture/perform that piece of music I composed/submit that poem for publication, I don't have to risk being rejected or criticized"

"If I never hand in that paper, I don't have to risk feeling bad when I see the red ink in the margins"

"If I never sign up for that advanced class, I don't have to risk the chance that I might not get as high a grade as I know I can if I stay where I am"

27

What are the two most noticeable words all these statements have in common? **Never** and **risk.** Many psychologists believe that the Superkid Syndrome is creating a generation of children who are afraid to take risks and fearful of not getting the approval they have been raised to appreciate. Many teachers are already concerned over the numbers of students who spend their school years calmly and obediently taking notes and following the rules — never questioning, never challenging, never speaking out.

There was once a shy writer who completed a huge manuscript but was afraid to turn it in to a publisher. What if no one accepted it? She wasn't sure she could take being turned down. Today there are 25 million copies of her book in print, around the world and in several languages. Her name was Margaret Mitchell; the name of her book was *Gone with the Wind.*

If you want to read more about some of the ideas in this chapter, try:

Procrastination: Why You Do It, What To Do About It by Jane Burka, Ph.D. and Lenora Yuen, Ph.D. (Reading, Massachusetts: Addison-Wesley Publishing Company, 1983)

Do It Now: How To Stop Procrastinating by Dr. William J. Knaus (Englewood Cliffs, New Jersey: Prentice-Hall, Inc., 1979)

Overcoming Procrastination by Dr. Albert Ellis and Dr. William J. Knaus (New York: New American Library, 1986)

CHAPTER 3

WHAT PERFECTIONISM DOES TO YOUR BODY

Are you a Type A person? Find out by reading the following statements. Respond to each with "I'm like that sometimes" or "I'm never like that."*

1. I feel hostile or angry much of the time.
2. I tend to talk, walk, and/or eat rapidly.
3. I'm extremely competitive.
4. I find myself scheduling more work into shorter time periods and leaving less time for play.
5. I often try to do two things at once — like eating and doing my homework, or talking on the phone and reading.
6. It's very hard for me to relax.
7. I'm impatient. For example, I HATE standing in lines.
8. I take pride in being able to do things faster and faster.
9. I seldom notice or take pleasure in beauty or nature.
10. I hardly ever listen to other people's opinions.

---

* Adapted from *Type A Behavior and Your Heart* by Dr. Meyer Friedman and Dr. Ray H. Rosenman (New York: Fawcett Crest, 1974). Reprinted by permission of the publisher.

If you answered "I'm like that sometimes" more often than you answered "I'm never like that," chances are you're a Type A person. In this case, the "A" isn't an award for excellence. Instead, it's a sign that you might be heading for trouble.

"Type A behavior" is a term that was coined by Drs. Meyer Friedman and Ray H. Rosenman to describe a very driven personality type. They found that Type A people had a greater-than-average chance of having high blood pressure, heart attacks, and strokes. Other studies have also shown that Type A people tend to be angry or hostile more often than others. They keep their feelings locked inside them until they boil over — and they hold grudges for a *long* time.

Is Type A behavior hereditary, or does it rub off on people? (In other words, if you spend a lot of time around Type A's, will you become one yourself? And are children of Type A parents more prone to being Type A's?) These are some of the questions researchers are asking today. Meanwhile, many hospitals are sponsoring workshops where Type A people can learn to slow down and ease up on themselves. And the War College at Carlisle, Pennsylvania is conducting workshops aimed at reducing the Type A behavior of its officers — without lessening their leadership ability.

Type A's have a lot of good qualities, like a high energy level and the ability to get things done. Many of them are leaders and hard workers. Many are also perfectionists.

In fact, Type A's and perfectionists have a lot in common. Here are some of the similarities researchers have uncovered:

■ A higher percentage of firstborn children are perfectionists — and a higher percentage of firstborn children are Type A's.

■ Both may have parents who are overly critical and controlling.

Parents of Type A's are often reluctant to let them try things on their own. Parents of perfectionists find it difficult to give them the freedom to experience trial-and-error learning.

■ Just as perfectionist children often have perfectionist parents, Type A children often have Type A parents.

And maybe those children grow up to be perfectionists and Type A's themselves . . . and raise still more perfectionists and Type A's.

■ Both tend to take on more and more activities and squeeze them into shorter and shorter time periods. Both think they can beat the clock.

■ Both are prone to stress-related illnesses from overloading their circuits and not getting enough rest.

In other words, it's not just the Type A's who are risking their health. Many perfectionists also pay for pushing themselves too hard and too fast.

The High Cost of the Confucian Work Ethic

We've heard a lot in recent years about the so-called "Japanese threat" to American business. Since World War II, "Made in Japan" has gone from being a sign of shoddy workmanship to a sign of quality, especially for high-tech items like automobiles, audio-visual equipment, and computers.

Not only are the Japanese super-productive in their work, they're also high achievers academically and intellectually. Part of this has to do with what's called the "Confucian Work Ethic." Asian-born students believe that they owe a great debt to their families, and the only way to repay it is by doing their best in everything. On the positive side, these students do tend to be exceptional performers. On the negative side, they feel tremendous guilt when they don't study as much as they think they should. They also seem more prone to stress-related illnesses and even suicide.

The Japanese have identified two diseases that are particular problems for their culture: *shinkeishitsu*, or "nervous temperament," and school phobia. Some of the symptoms of *shinkeishitsu* are perfectionism, hypersensitivity, social withdrawal, and intense discomfort in unfamiliar surroundings. School phobia may lead to fever, depression, and suicide. It accounts for almost half of the mental illness in Japan in people under the age of 18, and it can take up to two years of counseling and drug therapy to cure.

Why do so many Japanese students suffer from school phobia? Because they're subjected to *tremendous* pressure to perform and score high on tests — starting as early as kindergarten. Test scores are used to determine academic placement and tracking. Students who do well are placed in programs that lead to the high-status, high-security, and most desirable jobs; students who do poorly never have a chance at them. (Imagine what it would be like if a test you took in kindergarten determined your whole future!)

Perfectionist students in the United States have been known to show symptoms similar to those of *shinkeishitsu* and school phobia. They are also prone to other health problems, including headaches, migraines, muscle cramps, flu-like symptoms, stomach viruses, mononucleosis, gastro-intestinal problems, ulcers, sleep disorders, mood swings, depression, nervous tics, skin rashes, allergies, and exhaustion.

Some perfectionists suffer from a combination of physical, mental, and emotional problems. They literally make themselves sick.

"Speeding" Toward Trouble: Caffeine and Drugs

Have you ever wanted to stay awake when your brain and body told you it was time for bed? Have you ever felt that you *had* to stay awake — to study for a test, or finish a paper, or complete a project or presentation you were determined to get done before the morning?

Of course you have. We all have. Everyone gets behind on occasion, and everyone stays up too late once in a while, maybe even pulling an all-nighter.

For perfectionists, though, this can turn into a regularly scheduled event — especially if they combine their perfectionism with procrastination. They wait until the last minute to start something that will take hours to do. Then, when their heads start nodding over their desks, they reach for help.

pounding headache

nervous tic

crazed expression in eyes

buttons in wrong buttonholes

hammering heart

upset stomach

Coffee. Tea. Sodas. Over-the-counter stay-awake pills. These are the constant companions of the procrastinating perfectionist. The ingredient they all have in common is *caffeine.*

Caffeine is an odorless, slightly bitter alkaloid that acts as a stimulant to the nervous system. It increases your heart rate and rhythm, affects your circulatory system, and increases urination. It also stimulates the secretion of stomach acids. Too much can make you nervous, jittery, and cranky and upset your stomach.

Caffeine causes your body to release internal "stress signals" and produce "stress chemicals." That's why you can hear your heart beating and feel your adrenaline pumping. Normally your body only behaves like that when you're running away from something scary or climbing a mountain or performing some other fairly strenuous physical activity. If all you're doing is sitting and studying, the stress chemicals have nowhere to go. And that's when they start getting dangerous. Over a prolonged period of time, they can lead to ulcers, insomnia, high blood pressure, heart irregularities, heart disease, and delirium.

The perfectionist who's also a Type A may be in for double trouble, since Type As are already prone to diseases of the heart and circulatory system. They should be especially careful to stay away from caffeine, which may be hidden in all sorts of products — like cocoa, cold pills, and diet pills. When in doubt, read the label!

Caffeine has one thing going for it: at least it's legal. (One company has taken advantage of this to make a new cola called JOLT! with *twice* the caffeine of most carbonated soft drinks — just under the limits considered acceptable by the Food and Drug Administration. Three boos and a hiss for them!) There are other drugs that aren't legal, and some procrastinating perfectionists resort to these.

Truck drivers going on long runs have been known to take amphetamines, or "speed," to keep from falling asleep behind the wheel. Students studying for exams have been known to take them, too. At some schools, "speed parties" are considered cool.

Amphetamines obtained without a prescription are illegal in every state. But that's not the only reason to avoid them like the plague. They're dangerous, they're habit-forming, and their effects can be unpredictable.

One student took "speed" to get through the night before an important exam scheduled to last for three hours. He managed to stay up all night studying, but the next day was a disaster. He *thought* he was doing a great job when in fact he spent the entire three hours writing on the same line in his blue examination booklet. When he finally tore a hole in the paper, his professor had to drive him to the infirmary.

Healthy, well-rested, chemical-free people feel better, look better, and perform better. There's *never* a time when it's worth it to take drugs.

FIVE SAFE WAYS
TO STAY AWAKE

You've got to hand that paper in tomorrow morning at 9 sharp. Or you've **got** to study for that exam. No two ways about it — it's now or never.

Resist the urge to make a pot of coffee. Instead, try one or more of these **healthy** alternatives:

☐ Get physical.

Run in place, do situps or jumping-jacks, whatever. Exercise gets your heart pumping and moves oxygen-rich blood through your circulatory system. Plus it makes you feel better. After five or ten minutes of hopping around, you'll sit back down at your desk with pink cheeks and renewed energy.

☐ Turn on some stimulating music.

Sousa marches may be going too far, but rousing classical music or bouncy jazz may be just the ticket. Some students report that working to music actually improves their concentration because it shuts out other extraneous noises.

☐ Eat something crunchy and good-for-you.

Try cheese-and-crackers, a carrot, an apple, some celery sticks with peanut butter. Maybe your body needs a boost. (But stay away from sugar, which gives you a quick "high" and then sends you crashing down again.) Why crunchy? Because the noise you make chewing might help keep you awake!

☐ Meditate.

Find a comfortable place to sit; keep your spine straight; stare at a spot on the wall, or close your eyes; breathe slowly, deeply, and rhythmically; and think the same syllable, word, or short phrase over and over again. (Like listening to music, that has the effect of masking outside noises.) Whenever you find your mind wandering away from your syllable, word, or phrase (your "mantra"), get back on track with it. After about ten minutes of this, you should be able to return to work with a clear head.

☐ Take a catnap.

Set your alarm for a half-hour or an hour, then curl up under the covers and go to sleep. Even this short period of time will give your body and brain a chance to recharge.

The Eating Disorders Dilemma

When doctors and scientists study young people with eating disorders, they often find a common characteristic: perfectionism.

One recognized cause of eating disorders is the emphasis our culture places on the need to be thin at any cost. Television, advertising, and the movies are constantly sending the message that thin is in. Models are thin, stars are thin, gymnasts and dancers are thin. We've all heard the saying, "You can never be too rich or too thin," and many of us believe it. We equate thinness with physical perfection.

Two of the most severe eating disorders are *anorexia* and *bulimia.*

- **Anorexics** literally starve themselves through obsessive dieting, eating very little, or refusing to eat at all. They may make themselves vomit after eating or take diuretics or laxatives to keep their weight down.

- **Bulimics** "binge and purge," stuffing themselves with huge amounts of food and then forcing themselves to vomit.

Both disorders are dangerous, although anorexia is considered the more dangerous of the two. It has an estimated mortality rate of from 5-15 percent; it was the cause of singer Karen Carpenter's premature death.

Some of the side-effects of anorexia and bulimia include hypothermia, dehydration, insomnia, constipation, hair loss, and unclear thinking; women may find that their menstrual cycles become irregular or stop altogether. Damage to the esophagus and teeth may result from excessive vomiting, since vomiting brings up stomach acids. In extreme cases victims may experience damage to vital organs and heart failure.

While eating disorders occur in both sexes, females seem to be more susceptible than males; some sources estimate that 9 out of every 10 people who suffer from these disorders are female. It's further estimated that one out of every 20 teenage girls is anorexic, and that one out of every three women in the 18-to-30 age group is bulimic.

Anorexia and bulimia are complex disorders that operate on physical, emotional, and mental levels, which makes them especially hard to treat.

It's tough to convince the anorexic that he or she needs help. Often anorexics remain convinced that they're still "too fat" even when their ribs are sticking out and they're too weak to get out of bed. And bulimics usually binge and purge in secret.

Treatment for eating disorders includes hospitalization, counseling, behavior modification, and hypnosis. It's time-consuming and draining for everyone involved. Anorexics and bulimics fight back; parents feel guilty and frustrated.

For perfectionists, eating disorders are another side of the "all-or-nothing" mindset. The more you focus on being perfect, the more aware you become of your faults. Feelings of worthlessness set in. Especially if you think you're being dominated in other areas of your life — family, school, work — you may decide to take charge of at least one area: eating. Controlling and monitoring your food intake is something you *can* do.

Cathy Rigby McCoy was a talented gymnast who took 16th place at the 1968 Olympic Games in Mexico City. At the 1970 world gymnastics championships in Yugoslavia she became the first American woman to win the silver medal. She placed 10th at the Munich Olympics in 1972 and retired that year at age 19. She had already been bulimic for four years, and her problem continued when she started her new career in sportscasting and commercials. She remembers wanting to be a "perfect" team member and maintain a "perfect" weight. It wasn't until 1981 that she started getting professional help.

Ballerina Gelsey Kirkland starved herself periodically while a teenager and later learned to vomit to keep her weight down. At five feet four inches tall, she weighed less than 100 pounds. In her autobiography, *Dancing On My Grave,* she talks about her own pursuit of the body beautiful.

Several other famous women are making public their own bouts with anorexia and bulimia. Cherry Boone O'Neill, daughter of singer Pat Boone, describes hers in her book called *Starving for Attention.* Actress and political activist Jane Fonda was bulimic for many years. Actress Ally Sheedy was both bulimic and anorexic.

Many women with eating disorders admit to feeling pressured to be "the perfect person." Some lay the blame on parental expectations, while others point the finger at society and themselves. Often they share a deep fear of making mistakes and a low sense of self-esteem.

Eating disorders are a deadly way to try to gain control over your life. It's worth learning more about them. If you feel you need more information right away, you can contact either of the following:

- The Radar Institute specializes in treating eating disorders. Call them toll-free at 1-800-255-1818. Or write their main office: The Radar Institute, Trident Center, 11377 West Olympic Boulevard, Suite 555, Los Angeles, California 90064.

- The National Association of Anorexia Nervosa and Associated Disorders is a self-help organization with chapters or groups in most states. Call (312) 831-3438, or write: The National Association of Anorexia Nervosa and Associated Disorders, Affiliated with Highland Park Hospital, Box 271, Highland Park, Illinois 60035. You may request printed materials, but please send a self-addressed stamped envelope and $1 to help cover their printing and handling costs.

If you want to read more about some of the ideas in this chapter, try:

Type A Behavior and Your Heart by Dr. Meyer Friedman and Dr. Ray H. Rosenman (New York: Fawcett-Crest, 1985)

Is It Worth Dying For? A Self-Assessment Program to Make Stress Work For You Not Against You by Dr. Robert Eliot and Dennis L. Breo (New York: Bantam Books, 1984)

The Golden Cage: The Enigma of Anorexia Nervosa by Dr. Hilde Bruch (New York: Random House, 1979).

Starving for Attention by Cherry Boone O'Neill (New York: Dell, 1983).

Feeding the Hungry Heart: The Experience of Compulsive Eating by Geneen Roth (New York: New American Library, 1983).

CHAPTER 4

WHAT PERFECTIONISM DOES TO YOUR RELATIONSHIPS

Like most people, perfectionists need and want the friendship and approval of others. Yet they often have special problems in their family and social relationships.

Why? One reason is because they impose their too-high standards on everyone around them. Perfectionists believe that their friends, parents, teachers, and siblings have to be perfect, too. They have a bad habit of criticizing anyone who doesn't live up to their expectations or dares to make mistakes.

The trouble with criticism is that it alienates other people. Nobody likes being on the receiving end, and anyone who finds himself or herself in that position is likely to run the other way *fast*.

Let's say you've got a legitimate gripe. You want to get it off your chest, but you're not sure how to do it. In the past you've tried name-calling and stomping around, but something tells you those tactics don't work, so you're ready to try something new.

(Don't) You sound like you've got a built-in megaphone.

(Do) I really like what you have to say. I'd feel more comfortable though if you'd speak more softly.

Terrific! You've already take a giant step in the right direction.

What next? First of all, you should avoid criticizing people for *who and what they are* (or offer your biased interpretation of those facts). In other words, keep your comments off the personal level. For example, suppose you loan a friend a favorite shirt and it comes back with a spot on it. Shouting "You're a big slob with the table manners of an English sheepdog" is no way to open negotiations about the dry-cleaning bill.

Instead, try this three-step approach to problem-solving:

1. Clarify the issue in your own mind before bringing it up with the other person. Figure out what's really bothering you, then separate it out from issues that may be unrelated (like old gripes or grudges).

2. Tell the other person how you perceive the situation and how you feel about it — *without* accusing or criticizing. Avoid blanket statements like "You're *always* doing such-and-such" or "You *never* do so-and-so."

3. Propose a solution and give the other person the opportunity to do the same — while keeping an open mind.

For example, instead of "You're a big slob" etc., try "I'm glad you brought my shirt back, but I'm angry about the spot. I really want to wear it to my sister's wedding next Saturday. Do you think you could have it cleaned before then?"

OR INSTEAD OF THIS....

"You have a mouth the size of the Grand Canyon and it's obvious that I can't trust you anymore. You told Max the secret I told you. How could you do such a thing?"

...TRY THIS:

"Max told me something I was sure I told you in confidence. I feel angry and embarrassed about it. Maybe you didn't realize it was supposed to stay a secret. How can I let you know next time?"

INSTEAD OF THIS...

"You stole my idea for the science project. I guess you're too dumb to have ideas of your own, since you're always taking mine."

...TRY THIS:

"I was really surprised when you told the teacher what you wanted to do for the science project. It sounded a lot like the idea I told you about last week. If you needed help coming up with an idea, you could have asked me. Then I'd feel comfortable doing the same with you."

INSTEAD OF THIS...

"You're totally irresponsible. You promised to meet me at the game, and you didn't even show up. I waited around outside and missed the whole first quarter."

...TRY THIS:

"I thought we agreed to meet at the gym at 7:30. I felt silly standing there while everyone else walked past me to get inside. If something comes up the next time we make plans, could you call me at home and let me know?"

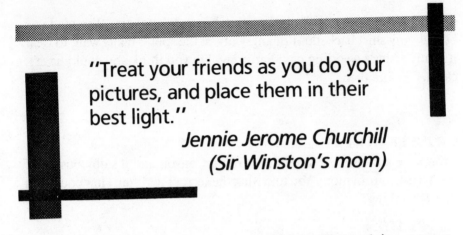

> "Treat your friends as you do your pictures, and place them in their best light."
>
> *Jennie Jerome Churchill*
> *(Sir Winston's mom)*

We could add a fourth and final step to this problem-solving process: forgiveness. In fact, that alone may be all that's necessary in some situations. The friend who goofs or lets you down may need to be told, "That's okay; forget it." Or "Yes, I was really angry (disappointed) about it, but I'm okay now and we can put it behind us."

Wanted: The "Perfect" Partner

Nowhere is the desire for "perfect" friends more apparent than when perfectionists go in search of partners — boyfriends and girlfriends.

What do *you* look for? When it comes to dating someone, what characteristics are important to you? For each of the following categories, choose a description from either the A or B column that comes closest to what you want in a partner.

1. Looks

A	B
A real knock-out . . . in great shape . . . cool clothes . . . when you walk down the street with this person, everyone notices	Someone who takes pride in his/her appearance . . . is comfortable with the way he/she looks . . . has his/her own personal style

2. Brains

A

Straight A-students only, please! . . . Has to be in the honors program . . . Someone who's at least as smart as I am

B

Has a lot of knowledge and insight into many different subjects . . . Seems curious about things; asks good questions . . . Knows things I don't know much about . . . is interesting to talk to

3. Popularity

Must be in the "in" crowd . . . a class officer . . . homecoming king/queen . . . captain of the football team/cheerleading squad . . . valedictorian . . . always invited to the best parties . . . a crowd-pleaser

Is liked and respected by others . . . knows how to make and keep friends

4. Personality

Outgoing . . . a real live-wire . . . always fun to be with

Fun to be with, but can also have a serious conversation . . . kind of quiet sometimes . . . doesn't talk unless he/she has something to say

5. Extracurriculars

Involved in the "in" clubs . . . always shows up at games . . . Prom Committee chair

Involved in the community . . . campaigns for political candidates . . . volunteers at the local hospital

You can probably see a pattern here. Column A descriptions have to do with more superficial characteristics that are dependent on popular opinion, while those in Column B focus more on inner qualities — the things that may not be as obvious and aren't as closely tied to what other people think.

The point is to ask yourself what you *really* want — and why. Have you decided that you'll only go out with straight-A students, or class officers, or the most popular students, or the best-looking ones? What about the guy/girl who's kind of shy, not too popular, and not a genius but seems interested in you? Are you willing to give that person a chance? How do you treat people who aren't as "good" as you are? Do you just tolerate them, or do you make a genuine effort to get to know them and let them get to know you?

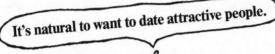

But if that's your only goal, you're bound to be frustrated and disappointed. It's when we learn to see what's under the surface that we stand the best chance of developing relationships that are meaningful, satisfying, and long-lasting.

Here's another area where the media don't help matters. If we accept what they say is important, it's hard to be ourselves and accept other people as they are, warts and all. In the movie "10," Dudley Moore pursues Bo Derek because she's a "perfect 10." In the movie "Perfect," the whole focus is on achieving the "perfect" body. Most of what Hollywood projects as perfection has to do with appearance alone — not personality, not abilities, not talents, but looks.

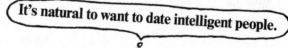

Especially if you're on the brainy side yourself, you'll prefer going out with someone at or near your own level. That way you're more likely to be able to find things to talk about and do that interest both of you. But there are many kinds of intelligence, not all of which show up on quarterly report cards and dean's lists. What about the B student who plays in a jazz band? Or the C student who's inventing intriguing gadgets in his or her basement after school?

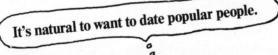

After all, going out with the class valedictorian, the class president, or the homecoming king or queen reflects on you. But when you limit your choices to a relatively few people (how many class presidents can there be?), you limit your chances to meet everyone else.

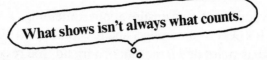

What shows isn't always what counts.

You get the idea. Take time to talk to the seemingly nondescript person who sits behind you in math class, and you might find someone who takes flying lessons . . . or runs marathons . . . or programs computers . . . or knows more about the woods than Davy Crockett. You'll never know unless you bother to find out.

You may never find the ideal partner — the "other half" we're all supposed to look for. But there are plenty of nice people out there who are worth meeting and spending time with.

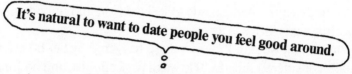

It's natural to want to date people you feel good around.

Another mistake perfectionists make is expecting to *always* feel great when they're with their boyfriends or girlfriends. But you can't turn this into an all-or-nothing proposition because it's unrealistic. It doesn't allow for off-days, mood shifts, and the ups and downs that are a normal part of everyday life and being human.

Most of us grew up hearing fairy tales in which the handsome prince and beautiful princess meet, get married, and live "happily ever after." Sad but true, there's no such thing. Relationships take work, and some of it isn't much fun. We have to be honest with others, and we have to be willing to listen when they're honest with us, even when it hurts.

It's equally unrealistic to expect another person to meet all of your emotional needs. Many young couples fall into this trap, getting so wrapped up in each other that they shut out the rest of the world and let their other friendships lapse. Even when you do find a partner who seems made for you, it's important to maintain your own interests, activities, and friendships outside of that relationship. (Besides, doing so makes *you* more interesting.)

When perfectionists do find partners, they may have a harder-than-usual time getting close to each other. They're reluctant to show their emotions and share information about themselves because they're afraid of being perceived as "imperfect." Getting close to others means taking risks and allowing people to know the *real* you — including the insecure and less-than-perfect parts.

It's okay to admit to being unsure about something . . . or worried . . . or even afraid. It's okay to show anger and frustration and disappointment. When you let your guard down in front of a friend, you're communicating your trust and confidence in him or her. And that tends to make friendships stronger.

Perfectionists are also prone to thinking they can change the people they get involved with. They seem to believe that others can't help but improve in their company — and they're all too willing to push the process along. "Let me make a suggestion" turns into "Do it *my* way." And "I hope you don't mind my telling you this, but . . . " is a sneaky way of saying, "Be the person *I* want you to be."

Nobody enjoys being made to feel inferior, and nobody is as skilled at projecting superiority as a perfectionist.

One young woman I know was so badgered by her boyfriend that she actually considered suicide. "He was a perfectionist, and nothing I did ever pleased him," she remembers. "I kept trying to meet his standards, but I never could. It drove me so crazy that I actually wrote a suicide note. Halfway through it I realized what I was doing and knew it was time to get out of the relationship. Now I look for people who accept me as I am."

> "The perfectionist is a man whom
> it is impossible to please because
> he is never pleased with himself."
> *Johann Wolfgang von Goethe*

Another problem some perfectionists have is the tendency to over-commit themselves and be super-responsible. They spend time on everything *but* their relationships. Overcommitment may be a way of avoiding closeness, and it may signal the need to reevaluate your priorities. It's important to keep your grades up, to get involved in outside activities, and to follow through on your promises and obligations. But it's also important to be there for your friends when they need you — especially if you expect the same from them.

"The only way to have a friend is to be one."
Ralph Waldo Emerson

How Parents can Make Things Worse

When perfectionists have problems in their relationships, it's seldom their fault alone. For many, the trouble starts at home with parents who want them to have "perfect" friends — meaning friends who meet *their* expectations.

Like the rest of us, parents sometimes forget that everyone has faults and blemishes, seen and unseen. While they usually do want what's best for their children, they can make mistakes. (Remember that they can also be right on occasion!)

Generally speaking, parents appreciate openness and knowing what's going on in their children's lives. It's when they're kept in the dark or surprised that they're apt to clamp down or make demands that seem unreasonable. If you want your parents to be more accepting of the friends you choose for yourself, here are some guidelines that might help:

■ Talk to them about the things you and your friends do together and why you enjoy being with them.

■ Try to respect and live within the boundaries your parents set for you.

If they decide that certain places and activities are off limits, don't just march off and do as you please. If they say no to something that's really important to you, present your case as calmly and objectively as you can. ("I know you don't like the pizza parlor. But that's where the chess club has decided to meet on Thursdays after school, and I really want to be in it this year.")

■ Don't keep your friends a secret — let your parents meet them.

Spend time with them at your house; invite them to dinner; give your parents a chance to see them and talk with them. It's easier to accept the known than the unknown.

Unless you plan to run off with the Hell's Angels, you should be able to pick your own friends. When it comes to your siblings, however, you're stuck with what you get. This is yet another area where parents can make a mess of things.

Even parents who know better can't help drawing comparisons between their children. It's when they do it aloud, however, that they fuel the fires of sibling rivalry. And when one child is a high-performance perfectionist, it can cause a rift that may take years to heal.

Siblings resent being measured against a brother or sister who seems to do everything right. As 15-year-old Andy reports, "My brother gets mad when Mom and Dad brag about my grades." Sheila, 14, feels cut off from her younger sisters: "My parents are always calling me 'the brain' and telling my sisters that they should be more like me. It's as if I'm the special one of the family and they're not important at all. That's not true, and I wish my parents would realize that I need to be a part of the family — not apart from it."

"My parents gave me everything I wanted," Ellen, 35, remembers. "My brother, on the other hand, was a C student. They'd barely even look at his report card before making a big deal about mine. He still hasn't forgiven me for that."

What can you do if your parents are being insensitive? You can try talking to them about it — always a good place to start. Maybe they honestly don't realize the effects of what they're doing.

You can also work extra hard at getting along with your siblings. Resist the temptation to remind them of how smart you are (even in the middle of an argument). Don't rub it in every time you succeed at something. Be

Wow, I didn't know you could do _that_... and you taught the cat, too?

sure to notice their achievements, and remain open to letting them show you a thing or two.

Finally, you can let them know that *you* don't like it when your parents compare them to you — that it makes *you* uncomfortable, too. Besides, it puts you in the position of having to be perfect all the time. They may think it feels good to spend your life on a pedestal, but it gets pretty lonely at the top.

If you want to read more about some of the ideas in this chapter, try:

Intimate Connections: How to Get More Love in Your Life by Dr. David Burns (New York: William Morrow and Company, 1984). See especially the chapter called "Liking and Loving Others: How to Overcome Romantic Perfectionism."

Bringing Up Parents: The Adolescents Handbook by Alex J. Packer (Washington, D.C.: Acropolis Books, Ltd., 1985). Discusses ways you can improve your relationship with your parents and work together to develop mutual trust and respect.

Why Am I Afraid To Tell You Who I Am? by John Powell (Illinois: Argus Communications, 1969).

CHAPTER 5

HOW TO EASE UP ON YOURSELF

Now that you know some of the side-effects of perfectionism, it seems only logical to remedy or avoid them. Since most of the pressure perfectionists feel comes from *inside,* a good place to begin is by easing up on yourself.

Maybe you need a role-model or two to start you on your way. Think of someone you admire — either from the past or from the present. If that person was (or is) famous enough to have warranted a biography, read it. Find out what his or her life was really like.

Charles Dickens, painter Claude Monet, dancer Isadora Duncan, and Mark Twain never finished grade school. Mary Baker Eddy, the founder of Christian Science, was a high-school drop-out — as were George Gershwin, Will Rogers, and both Wright brothers. So was newscaster Peter Jennings.

Emily Dickinson was a recluse. Martin Luther was intolerant of peasants and Jews. Charles Lindbergh was a reckless barnstormer who cracked up four planes before soloing across the Atlantic; prior to World War II, he came out in favor of the Nazis and recommended that America fight on the German side.

Tom Cruise, Bruce Jenner, O.J. Simpson, and Cher all have learning disabilities, as did Hans Christian Anderson, Nelson Rockefeller, Woodrow Wilson, and Leonardo da Vinci.

And lots of famous people stumbled and fumbled their way into the history books.

TEN FAMOUS PEOPLE WHO BLEW IT
(BUT LATER MADE IT BIG)

Madame Schumann Heink was told by an opera director that she "would never be a singer" and that she should "buy a sewing machine." She went on to star in the Imperial Opera in Vienna.

Babe Ruth hit 714 home runs — but he also struck out 1,330 times.

R.H. Macy failed seven times before making it big with his New York store.

Louisa May Alcott was told by an editor that she would never write anything popular. More than a century later, her novels are still being read, and the Children's Literature Association (an international group of librarians, teachers, authors, and publishers) considers *Little Women* one of the best American children's books of the past 200 years.

Walt Disney once got fired by a newspaper editor because "he had no good ideas." He went on to create Mickey Mouse, Donald Duck, the Disney Studios (which have won over 45 Academy Awards), and Disneyland; his greatest dream, EPCOT Center, opened in 1982.

Abraham Lincoln started out as a captain at the beginning of the Blackhawk War; by the end of the war, he had been demoted to private.

John Creasey, English novelist, got 753 rejection slips before publishing 564 books.

Charles Goodyear had many business failures and was even sent to debtor's prison before *accidentally* discovering the vulcanization process that revolutionized the rubber industry.

Thomas Edison's teachers called him "too stupid to learn." He made 3,000 mistakes on his way to inventing the lightbulb. Eventually he held 1,093 patents.

Lee Iacocca was fired from Ford Motor Company by Henry Ford II. He later became chairman of the board at Chrysler and headed the campaign to restore the Statue of Liberty. (He even bought Henry Ford's old house and moved in.)

What did these people all have in common, in addition to great ability?

They took risks. They took chances again and again. They took their failures in stride and kept on trying. They liked being challenged. They made mistakes and learned from them.

You can, too.

> "He who never made a mistake never made a discovery."
> *Samuel Smiles*

Learning to Fail

Perfectionists have a hard time taking risks. The fear of failure, of being "imperfect," is so strong it can be debilitating.

That's why one of the first things you should do to ease up on yourself is to try something new — something you've never done before, and preferably something you might not be very good at.

QUESTION: Isn't there a chance I won't succeed?
ANSWER: Of course there is.

QUESTION: Won't I look silly?
ANSWER: Maybe.

QUESTION: What if I can't do it perfectly?
ANSWER: That would be . . . *perfect.*

What's so good about performing badly — or, at least, less than perfectly? Here are just a few of the benefits:

- ■ It gives you a new perspective on yourself and everything else you do. (The first time you fall and pick yourself up and find that the world hasn't ended can be a liberating moment for the perfectionist.)

- ■ It gives you the freedom to strike out in still more untried directions.

- ■ It gives you a better understanding of others. (Whenever you try something outside your own realm, you can't help but look differently at people who know things you don't know and can do things you can't do.)

- ■ It gives you permission to do less-than-your-best at something else..and something else after that.

- It teaches you that there are *degrees* of accomplishment — that it's not an all-or-nothing proposition. (You don't have to be the best to learn something and have fun.)

- It teaches you that *not* succeeding can be normal, necessary, even desirable.

> "There is the greatest practical benefit in making a few failures early in life."
> *Thomas Henry Huxley*

So, what new something should you try? Make a list of things you've always been interested in. What about cross-country skiing, learning Russian, neon art, designing clothes, vegetarian cooking? What about sailing, sculpting, or modern dance? Why not develop a stand-up comedy routine? Anything you decide on will help you expand your horizons, discover more about yourself, stretch your brain, and come up with new criteria for self-assessment.

No matter what you choose, you can't lose.

I've always wanted to learn to fly. —

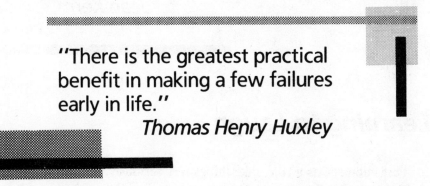

> "I think success has no rules, but you can learn a great deal from failures."
>
> *Jean Kerr*

Learning to Laugh

Perfectionists, as a rule, take things *very* seriously. It was probably a perfectionist who first coined the phrase, "Life is no laughing matter."

If you can't remember the last time you laughed so hard you cried or fell off your chair, you're long overdue. Start with safe things: funny movies, funny books, comedy records, cartoons. Hang around with funny people (chances are they won't be perfectionists — an excellent reason all by itself for seeking them out).

There are biophysical reasons why laughter makes you feel good. For one, it's terrific exercise. You simply can't keep still while you're doing it. Prolonged belly-laughter affects almost every muscle and most major organs. It increases your respiratory activity and heart rate, stimulates your circulatory system, and reduces stress. Meanwhile your pituitary gland releases chemicals that add to your sense of well-being. Your whole body feels lighter and more relaxed. (You may remember the scene from the movie "Mary Poppins" where people laughed, floated to the ceiling, and hung there like helium balloons. That's what it's like!)

Norman Cousins has been an anti-nuclear activist, a long-time editor of *Saturday Review* magazine, a personal emissary of Pope John XXIII, and the organizer of special projects for the victims of Hiroshima and the Holocaust. He believes that laughter actually saved his life. Twice he was diagnosed with near-fatal diseases; twice he checked into motels and watched the funniest movies he could find. (His favorites were slapstick comedies.) Both times he emerged feeling better than ever.

> "Laughter is by definition healthy."
> *Doris Lessing*

After you've practiced laughing at safe things, be brave and move on to the next stage: laughing at yourself. No derisive snorts or self-effacing giggles, please; what we're aiming for is honest laughter. What have you got to laugh at? Try to remember the last time you made a really silly mistake. (The longer ago you made it, the sillier it may seem.) Imagine how you looked from the outside. If someone you know had done the same thing, would you have laughed about it?

One of my most embarrassing moments was also one of the funniest. During college I was the featured baton twirler at football games. Once I dropped my fire baton on the field and started a small fire. Several band members marched over it in doubletime until they put it out. As they stomped on the fire, they kept on playing. I can still picture the scene, and it still makes me laugh.

> "When we can begin to take our failures nonseriously, it means we are ceasing to be afraid of them. It is of immense importance to learn to laugh at ourselves."
> *Katherine Mansfield*

Here are a few more ways to firm up your funnybone:

- Keep an imaginary library of "laugh tapes" in your head — incidents you've witnessed or been a part of, jokes you've heard, funny scenes from your favorite sitcoms. Then play a "tape" whenever you need a lift.

- Throw a party where everyone has to wear a silly costume. (An All-Vegetable party? A Come-As-Your-Favorite Alien dance? A "Leave-It-To-Beaver" party?)

- Read *Humor: Lessons in Laughter for Learning and Living* by Bernice Bleedorn with Sara McKelvey (Buffalo, New York: D.O.K. Publishers, 1984). It's packed with suggestions for making humor a habit. For example: Have a "Laughter Alert" by looking for unexpected and unscheduled humor. Plot and plan for laughter with jokes, gags, one-liners, puns, graphics, cartoons, illustrations, caricatures, smiles, riddles, parodies, and mime.

Getting Up and Getting Out

Too many all-nighters and too much stress can have a cumulative effect on your body. Laughter alone can't relieve it; what you need is *exercise*.

Instead of sitting around worrying about your GPA, try getting up and getting out. Widen your circle of friends to include active people. Then go camping, horseback riding, water-sliding, swimming, rafting, canoeing, rock climbing, ice skating, roller skating, bicycling — anything that sounds as if it might be fun. You'll come home with energy to spare, and your books will still be where you left them.

Whatever you choose, do it for the joy. Camping isn't about getting straight A's; it's about sleeping on the ground, singing around a campfire, roasting marshmallows, and trying to find the latrine in the dark. Nobody gives grades for water-sliding, that sport where *everyone* looks ridiculous. And a 4.0 average won't be much help the first time you climb into shoes with wheels.

Your fellow perfectionists may not be interested in such mundane activities. Even better, since that will give you the chance to meet new people. Tracy, 14, took a deep breath and joined her school ski club. Until then her only communication with the kids in it had been a few hellos in the hall. "They're really nice," she says, "and they *like* having a good time. Plus hardly anyone ever talks about grades. What a relief!"

Leave your competitive self at home with your books. If you turn your new pursuits into contests, you'll defeat their purpose. You don't have to be the best rock-climber or the swimmer with the most perfect form. You don't have to be the leader or the know-it-all. You'll probably be surprised at how wonderful it feels to relax and just be yourself.

Turning Problems Into Opportunities

Any problem becomes more manageable if you take the time to learn about it. Perfectionists know all about hitting the books and digging for facts; why not turn that to your advantage? Give yourself an assignment to study whichever aspect of perfectionism makes things hardest for you.

Are you an overachiever bordering on workaholism? Then read up on workaholism. Find out what doctors and researchers are discovering about its causes and its effects. Imagine that you're a counselor with a workaholic client, devise a treatment plan, and take your own advice!

Are you a procrastinator? Discover how other procrastinators are conquering this tendency. See whether one of your teachers will let you write a paper on it — and turn it in *on time.*

On the light side, you may want to get in touch with the Procrastinators' Club of America. The Club was founded in 1956 "to promote the fine art of procrastination to nonprocrastinators, to make known the benefits of putting things off until later, to honor those people who have performed exceptional acts of procrastination, and to have fun." Members have protested the war of 1812 and traveled to Spain to request three ships with which to discover America. Meetings are irregular and late. Request a copy of their *Last Month's Newsletter,* but don't hold your breath waiting for it. Write or call: Procrastinators' Club of America, Inc., 1111 Broad-Locust Bldg., Philadelphia, PA 19102, (215) 546-3861.

Do you suffer from writer's block? Learn all you can about it. Ironically, quite a lot has been written on the subject — by writers, of course. There are entire books on writer's block waiting for you at your public library. For example:

- *Right Brain . . . Write On! Overcoming Writer's Block and Achieving Your Creative Potential* by Bill Downey (Englewood Cliffs, New Jersey: Prentice-Hall, Inc., 1984).

In *The Complete Handbook for Freelance Writers* (Cincinnati: Writer's Digest Books, 1981), Kay Cassill cites six reasons for creative blocking and burnout. Two will come as no surprise to the dedicated perfectionist: Setting Expectations Too High, and Taking Too Little Time To Play. In *How To Write and Sell Your Personal Experiences* (Writer's Digest Books, 1986), Lois Duncan recommends, "The first thing to do when you find yourself a victim of writer's block is to accept it for exactly what it is: not the end of the world, but a rejuvenation period. *Let* yourself rest . . . Go to lunch with friends, give a party, play tennis, take a little trip, attend lectures, go to the zoo, take a hike, go dancing."

Never underestimate the power of a challenging assignment to get you excited and lead the way toward solutions. If there's one thing perfectionists are *really* good at, it's leaving no stone unturned. In their push to make sure to get everything right, they do a thorough job of gathering information and ferreting out facts.

When I discovered that my biggest problem was perfectionism, I decided to tackle it head-on. I made it the subject of my doctoral dissertation. I even wrote a book about it; you're reading it now.

If you want to read more about some of the ideas in this chapter, try:

Human Options by Norman Cousins (New York: Berkley Books, 1983)

Mistakes Are Great! by Dan Zadra with Bob Moawad (Mankato, MN: Creative Education, 1986)

CHAPTER 6

A SPECIAL MESSAGE FOR GIRLS AND YOUNG WOMEN

It's no secret that females have traditionally been raised to be non-assertive, accepting, and complacent. Things are changing, but progress is slow. Even today most women hesitate to make waves, and most work hard to be agreeable.

Many women find it difficult to say no to requests, pleas, and demands for their time. If they also have perfectionist tendencies, it's easy to see how they can get overbooked and stretched to their limits.

During her junior year in high school, Cynthia woke up one day and realized that she was an officer in five school clubs, president of her class, head of the homecoming float committee, taking a full load of accelerated courses, and participating in after-school piano, dance, and French lessons. She pulled her covers over her head and wailed, "How did this happen to me?" She managed to make it to the end of the year, which was also nearly the end of her rope. Afraid to disappoint the people who were counting on her, she pushed herself to her limits.

It may sound selfish, but there are times when it's necessary to look out for Number 1. That means learning how to say no. That means taking time to rest, recuperate, and review after finishing one set of projects and before starting the next. That means slowing down, calming down, and taking stock of where you are and where you *really* want to go.

It's great to be able to do many things well, but overdoing it to the point of being stressed-out and worn out is taking it too far. I've known several young women who have landed in the hospital with severe exhaustion. Determined to be all things to all people, they neglected someone important — themselves.

Taking on more than you can handle can have results you didn't anticipate. You may find yourself unable to do your best work or even to perform competently. In trying to do *everything,* you may end up doing *nothing* you can be proud of. (Especially if you're flat on your back in a hospital.)

Thanks in large part to the women's movement, women today are being more assertive and outspoken than ever before. As more are promoted into management positions (or start their own businesses), they're learning to delegate responsibility and authority to others. Many do this reluctantly, however, especially if they're perfectionists. There's always the unspoken fear, "What if the person I gave this job to isn't as 'perfect' as I am?" For perfectionist women, delegating is a three-stage struggle. First they must work to trust the other person; then they must actually make the assignment; and then they must be willing to accept the consequences. Not everyone can do as good a job as a perfectionist, and that fact is hard to swallow.

Some perfectionists manage the first two stages and then backslide, redoing the project they assigned until it meets their own high standards. This in turn leads to burnout — not to mention bad feelings on the part of the person whose work is redone.

"A perfectionist is someone who takes great pains and then gives them to others."

Anonymous

Ironically, the goals of the women's movement have been misinterpreted as putting extra pressure on women to perform. Since its inception, the movement has been about the freedom to make choices, especially in areas that have long been closed to women. It has never been about being "perfect" at home *and* on the job. In fact, it's nearly impossible to have a gorgeous house, a brilliant career, and well-behaved, perpetually spotless children unless you also have a staff of servants (or a magic wand).

Women in the 1950s — the decade in which television became widely available — learned from the ads that they were supposed to have "perfect" houses, cook "perfect" meals, look "perfect" and raise "perfect" children. Women in the 1980s are hearing all this, *plus* they're being told that they must be "perfect" at work, compete with men, and climb the corporate ladder as fast as they can. Young women are looking ahead and wondering, "Can I do it?" Many are already feeling unequal to the monumental task of doing it all.

Here's the good news: You don't have to. And you can start now learning how to keep your life in balance.

Tips For Avoiding Burnout — Now and Later

First, learn how to say no. Practice it in front of the mirror. Practice saying it without reservation, without hesitation, in an "I-mean-it" tone of voice. Then use your newly-acquired skills at your earliest opportunity.

Lila, 15, was amazed at how she felt the first time she said it. "When the editor of our school newspaper moved to another state, I got a call asking me to take his place. I wanted to do it, but I knew I already had enough to handle for the rest of the term. So I said no. The next day I got another call asking if I had changed my mind. I said no again. I felt exhilarated and full of energy and power. It was great!"

Second, start prioritizing your activities so you can space them out more efficiently. If possible, get hold of a large wall calendar you can write on, erase, and write on again (you may change your mind more than once during this process). Mark down your most important activities and label them with the number 1. Then mark down the second-most important activities, label them with the number 2, and so on. When you've finished — and make sure to include *everything,* from student council meetings to term-paper due-dates to dances — look closely at the results. If at all possible, start eliminating those with the highest number and work backwards, erasing as many as you can. Leave at least one or two nights a week for yourself and whatever *you* choose to do whenever *you* choose to do it. Be spontaneous! Be imaginative! Be silly!

Third, take a few lessons from the boys and men you know. Maybe you've heard your father say, "I'm sorry, I can't agree to do that right now. I'm already doing as much as I have time for." Or maybe you've heard a brother or boyfriend turn down an invitation because he needed an evening to sit around or a morning to sleep in. Have you noticed that they seldom sound apologetic when they refuse a request?

> "Women are brought up to be selfless. A man is brought up just the opposite — to do what's best for himself first."
> *Triathlete Gayelene Clews*

There's something else to be learned from males: the ability to express anger and let it go. Studies have found that more women than men are subject to bouts of depression, and there are theories suggesting that it's because women turn their anger inward while men turn theirs outward. Boys seem able to vent their feelings in a blast and then go on as if nothing has happened, while girls tend to stew for days or weeks or months.

Instead of repressing, try saying "I'm angry!" and doing something to let your anger out. Jog around the block, yank weeds out of the garden, pound a pillow. (It sounds silly, but it works.)

While you're at it, why not practice releasing some of the other feelings you may have kept locked inside — like jealousy, fear, sadness, anxiety, and doubt? If you don't believe you have these feelings, you may want to have a talk with an adult you trust — like a parent, a pastor or rabbi, or a school counselor.

Regardless of what you may have heard, *you don't have to be happy, cheerful, and smiling all the time.* Many girls are still brought up believing that this is how they should behave in any and all circumstances. Not true! You're entitled to be as grumpy as your brother, as gloomy as your dad, as grouchy as your boyfriend sometimes is — as long as that's the way you really feel. People may be surprised by the new you, but don't let that stop you. They'll get used to it; give them time.

From Superkid to Superwoman

The Superkid Syndrome discussed in Chapter 1 has a grown-up counterpart: the Superwoman Syndrome. Just as children are being pushed to achieve more sooner, women are being pushed to do everything competently and cheerfully. You've seen the ads: Mom bursts through the door, briefcase in hand, and races to the stove to whip up dinner. By the time it's ready she has miraculously changed into a gorgeous dress, put the children to bed, set a beautiful table, and lit the candles.

Even the "real" Superwoman never took on the responsibilities of a family. She flew around saving the world, but she never had to plan fourteen meals a week and pack school lunches, do the laundry, and go to PTA meetings.

Many young women are already worrying about their ability to function as Superwomen in the 1990s. Will they be able to pull it off? What will they have to sacrifice — time to themselves? their personal interests? a social life? Is it really possible to do it all?

A better question might be: *Is it really desirable?* It's not too soon to start thinking about where you want to be in five years, or ten, or twenty. Remember that you're not necessarily making plans — you're only exploring possibilities. Again, you may want to talk to your school guidance counselor. Then talk to adult women you know and admire — teachers, neighbors, your mom. Learn about the choices other women are making. Ask a librarian to point you toward books and articles about women.

A good place to begin is with a book called *Smart Girls, Gifted Women* by Barbara Alane Kerr, Ph.D. (Columbus, Ohio: Ohio Psychology Publishing Co., 1985). Kerr describes several successful women who started out as gifted girls with perfectionist tendencies: scientist Marie Curie; writer Gertrude Stein; anthropologist Margaret Mead; artist Georgia O'Keeffe; opera star Beverly Sills; writer, dancer, and political activist Maya Angelou. These women were often impatient with mediocrity. They felt driven toward excellence and were able to integrate several roles into their lives. Some were wives and mothers, and all were friends, as well as being leaders in their fields.

Until recently, perfectionism in women has followed a somewhat different path than perfectionism in men. For women, it has been tied primarily to family, home, and personal appearance, while for men it has been linked to performance in the workplace. That appears to be changing. More women are striving to succeed at home *and* at work, and the combination is resulting in added stress and strain.

After one month as president of the Philippines, Corazon Aquino said, "I am learning to say no." That may be the most important thing any woman today can learn.

If you want to read more about some of the ideas in this chapter, try:

The Type E Woman: How to Overcome the Stress of Being Everything to Everybody by Harriet Braiker (New York: Dodd, Mead & Co., 1986)

The Angry Book by Theodore I. Rubin (New York: Macmillan Books, 1970)

WAYS TO REALLY (and realistically, and responsibly) GAIN CONTROL OVER YOUR LIFE

It's the night before your research paper is due. You're sitting at your desk surrounded by piles of paper, stacks of books, scribbled-on note cards, chewed-up pencils, empty pop cans, and eraser crumbs. You look at your watch . . . midnight. You look at the piece of paper sticking out of your typewriter . . . blank.

You're in BIG trouble.

Things are OUT OF CONTROL.

How did they reach that point? You knew about this paper a month ago, and somehow you let it slide. And it's not the first time you've found yourself in this fix.

But it could be the last. You *can* take control of your life — *without* giving in to your perfectionism. The secret lies in recognizing what you can and can't control.

A clergyman named Reinhold Niebuhr said it best in a prayer he composed in the 1930s: "O God, give us serenity to accept what cannot be changed, courage to change what should be changed, and wisdom to distinguish the one from the other."

There are things you *can't* change — like the deadline for your research paper. And there are things you *can* change — like the way you go about trying to meet it.

Tried-and-True Ways to Get Things Done

Anything is easier if you break it down into bite-sized pieces. For example, you've been told to write 20 pages on some aspect of life in the Ice Age. You can think of it as a stack of paper 1/8" high crying out to be filled with somewhere around 3,000 words (aargh!) — or you can think of it as several manageable steps to be accomplished in a logical order.

Like this:

STEP 1. **Choose your focus.** Is there anything you're particularly interested in — such as art, religion, where in the world Ice Age families lived, how they built their homes, what they wore, or what they ate? Maybe you can center your paper around that.

Chloe, 16, likes to write and read poetry. Asked to write a paper on contemporary life in India, she decided to approach the subject by reading some of its poets in translation. She was able to use their firsthand observations of their culture as the basis of her paper — and she got to do something she enjoys (read poetry).

Erik, 15, has always been fascinated by bridges. Given an assignment to write about an old European city, he chose Venice — a city of more than 400 bridges.

STEP 2. **Compile a bibliography of journals and books pertaining to your topic.** One or two afternoons at the library can yield more sources of information than you may ever need — especially if you know where to look. *The Reader's Guide to Periodical Literature* is an obvious (and excellent) resource for articles, but don't stop there. Your librarian can point you toward all kinds of reference books and specialized indexes.

For a thorough introduction to research and writing methods, read *The Modern Researcher* by Jacques Barzun and Henry F. Graff (New York: Harcourt Brace Jovanovich, Inc., 1985).

STEP 3. **Take careful notes on what you read.** You can scribble them in a spiralbound notebook (and spend hours later searching through them), or you can write them on cards. Cards are much easier to organize and reorganize as ideas start forming in your mind. Invest in some 5 x 8" notecards — much roomier than the usual 3 x 5" variety. Use them to jot down any paragraphs, sentences, or brilliant turns of phrase that come to you along the way.

STEP 4. **Write an outline based on your notes.** The more detailed the better, because then all you'll have to do is . . .

STEP 5. **Fill in the blanks between the items on your outline.** In other words, if you complete steps 1-4, you'll be well on your way to having that paper done — on time.

Psychologist A.L. Lakein calls this the "Swiss cheese" method. You "punch holes" into big projects by dividing them into smaller and more manageable sections. When you're ready to start writing, you should have punched so many holes into your assignment that it looks like Swiss cheese.

Breaking a project down in this way makes sense. So how are you going to make sure that you actually *do* it? Try getting permission from your teacher to hand in each part as you complete it. This will give you a push in the direction of finishing the different items on schedule — and it may also give you the benefit of being able to discuss your work-in-progress with your teacher.

If that isn't possible, draw up a contract with *yourself.* Set a deadline for each part, then meet it! Build in some rewards for good behavior. Some possibilities: going for a bike ride after you finish your research, or watching a movie when you're done with your outline.

Your contract might look something like this:

Ice Age Paper Due Friday, February 20!!!

1. Choose focus by Monday, February 2

2. Go to library after school on Wednesday and on Saturday morning (plan to spend whole day there if necessary)

3. Organize notes by Tuesday, February 10 (SKATING PARTY that night)

4. Do outline by Thursday, February 12 and talk about with teacher during study hall

5. Start writing paper on Friday after school (MOVIE WITH LISA AND TOM at 7:00) Try to get first two pages done!

6. Write AT LEAST another five pages on Saturday

7. Have paper halfway done by Tuesday, February 17

8. HAND IN on Friday morning (CONCERT that night — HAVE FUN!)

I promise to stick to this schedule — no excuses!

Signed:

Once you've signed your contract, stick to it. You'll be surprised at how easy it is to move from step to step. Resist the urge to procrastinate, no matter how strong it is. Ten minutes in front of the TV can turn into three hours . . . five minutes with a mystery novel can become an all-night page-turner.

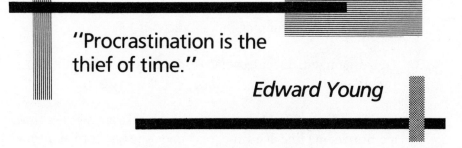

What if you get stuck? *Really* stuck — as in paralyzed, empty-headed, and desperate? You've written ten pages, and suddenly *you don't like them.* Should you tear them up, throw away the scraps, and start over?

Maybe — and maybe not. First, ask yourself why you don't like them. Is it because they aren't perfect? Or do they just need a little cosmetic surgery?

In his book, *Mindstorms: Children, Computers, and Powerful Ideas,* Seymour Papert, Ph.D. discusses something he calls the "debugging concept." He applies it specifically to computer programming, but like any good idea it translates across several disciplines.

Dr. Papert explains that someone who is writing a computer program should never ask "Is it right?" or "Is it wrong?" but rather "Is it fixable?" Few (if any) computer programs run flawlessly the first time. Instead of erasing it and starting over, it's far preferable to try to fix it — or "debug" it, in computerese.

See if you can find the "bug" in your paper. Or mark the specific sentences or paragraphs that "bug" you the most. Then go to work fixing them, one at a time.

Word processors are terrific tools for mistake-prone humans. So are white-out and correcting tape. So are scissors and Scotch tape; you can "cut & paste" your paper together, then photocopy it and hand in the photocopy (provided your teacher will accept it; check first!).

Whether you're writing a paper, preparing a Chopin nocturne for your senior recital, learning your lines for the school play, or training for a marathon, there are always two ways to perceive a task: as a horrible whole, or as a series of parts to be completed one after another. And there are always five steps you can take to get through it:

1.   Choose your focus.

2. Gather all the materials you need to get the job done. (Sharp pencils. A piano. Your running shoes. Whatever.)

3. Get organized. Decide what to do first, second, third . . . twenty-third.

4. Divide and conquer. Do one part at a time, take one step at a time, memorize one line at a time, play one note or chord at a time. Then move on to the next, and the next, and the next until — surprise! — you're through.

5. Even if your performance isn't perfect, don't stop until you've completed the first draft, the first run-through, the first read-through. You can always go back later and smooth out the rough spots.

Setting Reasonable Standards for Yourself

Your assignment is to write on some aspect of life in the Ice Age. Your assignment is *not* to write a definitive study suitable for publication in a scholarly journal, nor is it to one-up Jean Auel's *Clan of the Cave Bear.*

You don't always have to be the best and the brightest. Sometimes it's enough just to do a competent job. That's one of the hardest things for the hard-core perfectionist to learn — especially in a society as competitive as ours.

The need to compete makes people do strange things. Some athletes use (illegal) steroids to promote muscle growth, risking dangerous side-effects later in life. Some students are so determined to be first in every subject that all they do is study — and literally ace themselves out of admission to many colleges, which look for evidence of well-roundedness (including an active social life).

There are many people who didn't come in first, yet came out ahead in the long run. Cloris Leachman, Betty Buckley, Nancy Moore Thurmond, and Susan Anton all competed in the Miss America Pageant, and none of them won. But Leachman went on to become an award-winning actress; Buckley won a Tony for her performance in the Broadway musical "Cats;" Thurmond became a columnist and civic leader; Anton won fame as an actress, nightclub performer, and commercial spokesperson. And almost nobody remembers who "beat" them in the pageant.

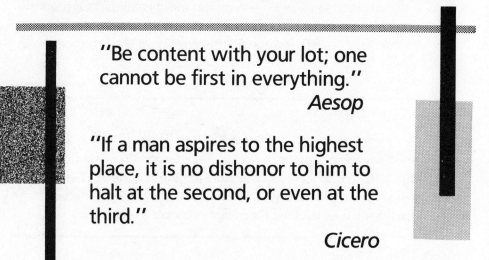

"Be content with your lot; one cannot be first in everything."
Aesop

"If a man aspires to the highest place, it is no dishonor to him to halt at the second, or even at the third."
Cicero

Avis is famous for its second-place position. E.B. White's wonderful children's book, *Charlotte's Web,* didn't win the Newberry Award in 1953, but it's a lot better known than *Secret of the Andes,* which did.

Buzz Aldrin wasn't the first man on the moon, but he never complained about following Neil Armstrong down the landing-module ladder into history.

RIDDLE

What do you call someone who graduates in LAST place in his or her class in medical school?

ANSWER:
A doctor.

In any contest, there's only *one* first place and *one* last place. In between is a wide middle range, with plenty of room to explore, experiment, and experience your possibilities. Setting too-high standards for yourself prevents you from ever finding this middle range and all the surprises it holds.

You don't have to do everything right all the time. In fact, it's usually preferable to do things *on time* — even if it means making compromises with yourself. Faced with the choice between turning in a paper that doesn't completely satisfy you and not turning one in at all, the *best* choice is always the former.

TIP

Most papers and projects usually take longer than you think they will. Try to include extra time in your schedule. Then, if you surprise yourself by finishing sooner than you planned, you'll have time left over for things you want to do.

Gunther Klaus, Ph.D., heads the Institute for Advanced Planning in Beverly Hills, California, a management think-tank that consults to corporations around the world. He offers these words of wisdom: "Getting things accomplished on time is far more important than perfecting them. Imperfection has been with us since the beginning of mankind. But inventors, creators, and manufacturers have always recognized that there is room for improvement — later."

Planning Positive Alternate Paths

Scientists, inventors, and other creative types know that there's usually more than one solution to a problem. They learn to leave themselves an "out" in case a particular approach leads nowhere or they get bogged down. They become adept at shifting gears, changing directions, and planning *positive alternate paths* — different ways to go in the event of a dead end or an unforeseen discovery.

- In 1608, a Dutch spectacle maker named Hans Lippershey was holding a lens in each hand when he happened to look through both of them at the same time. The result? He invented the telescope.

- In 1895, a German scientist named Wilhelm Konrad von Roentgen laid a Crookes tube on a book before going to lunch. (A Crookes tube produced cathode rays — streams of electrons.) What he didn't know was that the tube was activated, there was a key tucked inside the book, and the whole arrangement was sitting on a piece of photographic film. Later he developed the film and found the image of the key. He had taken the first X-ray — by mistake.

- In 1872, an American photographer named Thomas Adams was working hard to create a substitute for rubber. He had acquired a lump of gum from the chicle tree to experiment on, and one day he put some in his mouth and started to chew. He later made a fortune on the fruits of his discovery — chewing gum.

- In 1904, an anonymous lady in St. Louis was handed an ice-cream sandwich and a bouquet of flowers by her friend, Charles E. Menches. Menches had neglected to bring a vase, so she took one layer of the sandwich and rolled it into the shape of a vase, then did the same with the other layer and used it to hold the ice cream. She had invented the first ice-cream cone.

THE POST-IT NOTES STORY: HOW FAILURE TURNED INTO SUCCESS

You've seen them everywhere: those little yellow notes you can write on, stick to almost any surface, leave on for as long as you like, then remove without doing any damage. They're called Post-it Notes, they're made by the 3M Company of St. Paul, Minnesota, and they're one of the top 10 best-selling office products of all time.

But nobody at 3M ever started out to invent Post-it Notes. In fact, the man responsible for them, scientist Art Fry, was supposed to be working on something else (a shelf arranger for libraries) when he made his discovery.

One day in 1974 Fry was singing in the choir of his church, North Presbyterian in St. Paul, puzzling through a problem. Whenever he marked the pages of his hymnal with pieces of paper, they fell out, and when he got up to sing he couldn't find his place. He wondered if it might be possible to put adhesive on a bookmark.

3M had already developed an adhesive that Fry thought might work. Actually, the adhesive he had in mind was an accidental byproduct of other research, and no one at 3M liked it because it didn't stick very well.

Sneaking time from his other projects, Fry started working on his idea. His supervisor, Bob Malinda, helped find the money Fry needed to do a trial manufacturing run. Fry and others who believed in Post-its started passing out "pilot pads" to people within the company.

They caught on fast. People who used them wanted more. Post-its, it turned out, were habit-forming.

It took a long time for Fry and his supporters to convince 3M's management to put its manufacturing and marketing resources behind the new product. When they finally did, it was a smashing success that's now resulting in millions of dollars in sales each year.

Not bad for a "failed" adhesive and a man who should have been inventing shelf arrangers.

How can you plan positive alternate paths? Here are some suggestions:

1. Try to get comfortable with uncertainty and ambiguity.

This is very difficult for perfectionists, who are usually so *un*comfortable leaving anything to chance that they plan their lives months in advance.

Leave some room for unplanned events — spontaneous discoveries, sudden decisions. If the thought makes you very uneasy, start small. Take a walk one day without planning where you'll go or how long you'll be gone. Just walk, following whatever route interests you even slightly. When you start getting tired, turn around and head back. Then jot down a few of the surprises you saw along the way.

2. Give yourself permission to make mistakes.

This is another terrifying prospect for perfectionists, who equate mistakes with abject failure and being "no good."

Some of the best ideas have come out of goofs, bloopers, and outright accidents. Mistakes can be positive learning experiences, *if* you let yourself learn from them. Many perfectionists deny their mistakes, cover them up, or (even worse) refuse to try anything new for fear of making a mistake. They keep traveling the same old risk-free paths over and over again.

But a mistake can be a wonderful thing. It stimulates your curiosity ("what went wrong, and where?") It sparks your investigative skills ("hmm, let's look at *this* and dig into *that* and see if we can find some answers"). It spurs your creative energies ("I think I'll try *this* . . . and if it doesn't work, I'll try *that*"). And it adds to your store of useful experience ("at least I know not to do it *that* way again").

> **"Mistakes are a fact of life. It is the response to error that counts."**
> *Nikki Giovanni*

3. Be flexible.

To plan — and follow — positive alternate paths, you have to be willing to step off the one you're on. And that can be scary.

It can also be exciting. Who knows what you'll discover . . . who knows where you'll end up.

Christopher Columbus went in search of India and found America. Lyndon Baines Johnson started out as a schoolteacher and became the 36th president of the United States. Sally Ride wanted to be an astronaut as a child, but she never thought it would be possible. So she decided to do the next best thing: get a Ph.D. in astrophysics and join the space program as a scientist. (She also became a top-ranked college tennis player.) Then the call came from NASA that changed her life.

4. Give yourself time.

There are some positive alternate paths you can't plan. They come to you like bolts of lightning, "aha" experiences that point toward solutions you might not come up with in a million years.

That's not planning. That's *inspiration.*

The great inventor Thomas Alva Edison once said, "Genius is one per cent inspiration and ninety-nine per cent perspiration." What he didn't say is that inspiration isn't necessarily "on call" 24 hours a day. In other words, you can't just sit down at your desk, grab a pen, and say, "Okay, I'm ready!"

For centuries artists have personified inspiration and called it by name: the Muse. The Muse has been characterized as a woman-spirit who comes and goes pretty much as she pleases. If you're not ready when she is, you lose!

In her poem, "Levitation with Baby," Marilyn Nelson Waniek describes what happens when a busy mother receives a visit from the Muse. The mother agrees to accompany the Muse — but first she has to pack the baby's favorite toys and books, grab some diapers and plastic bags, prepare a lunch, feed the baby, clean up after him, wipe his fingers, fix a couple of bottles, change the baby, and wash her hands. Finally she says, "I'm ready." But it's too late — the Muse is gone.*

---

* If you want to read "Levitation with Baby," you can find it in Marilyn Nelson Waniek's book, *Mama's Promises* (Baton Rouge: Louisiana State University Press, 1985).

When you schedule every second of your life, you don't leave room for the Muse. Inspiration often comes in quiet moments — moments when you let your mind wander freely. You may have noticed that some of your best ideas pop into your head just as you're falling asleep at night, when you've finally let go of your hold on your brain. Why not leave space during the day as well?

The 3M company, makers of Post-it Notes and countless other successful products (like Scotch tape and Magic Tape, to name just two) knows how important it is to give people time to think. They have a policy that allows employees to work on projects of their own choosing for 15 percent of their time. Called "bootlegging," it has led to many interesting (and profitable) discoveries and inventions — Post-it Notes being just one.

Try some "bootlegging" of your own. Set aside half an hour a day — or an hour, or even two — for pursuing your own interests, apart from schoolwork or extracurriculars. See what happens when the Muse can find you and you've got time to listen.

Or, if you prefer, go looking for her. The Muse tends to hang around art and artists — the evidence of her influence, and the people who heed it. Take a Saturday afternoon to wander around a gallery or a museum. Spend a morning reading poems or short stories. Go to a classical music concert or watch a painter at work. Page through an art book.

Can't figure out what to do with that Ice Age paper? Wander through some pictures of the famous painted caves at Lascaux, France: the ant-

lered deer and wild cattle on the walls, the black-and-red horses on the ceiling. Imagine the people who painted them. The caves are pitch-black inside, so they must have carried some sort of light — probably lamps filled with animal fat, with moss for wicks. Imagine the light flickering across the cave walls, and how the animals painted there must have looked as if they were moving. Close your eyes and smell the burning fat from the lamps, and feel the soft fur of your bison cloak . . . .

Now you're ready to write!

> "The most beautiful thing in the world is, precisely, the conjunction of learning and inspiration. Oh, the passion for research and the joy of discovery!"
>
> *Wanda Landowska*

Getting to Know the Real You

If someone came up to you and said, "Tell me about yourself," how would you answer? With a long description of *what you do?* Or with a verbal picture of *who you are?*

People in the United States often define themselves by their occupations. Go to any gathering of adults and you'll hear what sound like ritual conversations: "Hello, I'm so-and-so . . . What do you do?" "I'm a lawyer/ doctor/ teacher/ homemaker/ I have my own business/ I'm a student" — and so on. We derive our identities from our jobs.

That may be one reason why so many people die so soon after they retire. Once they lose their jobs, they lose their sense of themselves. They're nobody if they're not *doing* something.

There's nothing wrong with being proud of what you do, but within reason, please! And what about the rest of you? Don't you want people to know more about you than the fact that you're class president, get straight A's, or are in your fourth year of Advanced Slovenian at the university?

Wouldn't it be nice if, instead of introducing you as "the smartest kid in class," someone introduced you as being humorous, kind, thoughtful, brave, and a good person to have as a friend?

It's hard to break old habits. But the next time someone asks you, "What do you do?" try responding in a completely different way than you're used to. Say, "I read old Krazy Kat comics," or "I listen to fusion jazz," or "I stargaze," or "I watch Alfred Hitchcock movies." You're still talking about what you do, but in a brand-new way. By giving people a glimpse into your interests, you're giving them a glimpse into *you.* And that can lead to some interesting conversations.

Getting to know the real you also means allowing yourself to have all the emotions you're capable of. And that means experiencing *and express-ing* a wide range of feelings — including "imperfect" ones like anger, aggression, jealousy, and fear. Many perfectionists grow up believing that they have to be "good boys" and "good girls." They're told not to cry, not to get mad, not to shout, not to feel sorry for themselves, not to complain. "Imperfect" feelings may not fit your image of yourself, but they're there anyway, and you know it. Unless you're from the planet Vulcan, you *need* to let them out. Keeping them locked inside leads to unhappiness, stress, and in extreme cases emotional illness. Find constructive outlets for the feelings you can't talk about. Instead of turning your anger inward, yell, scream, kick a can, or hit something. Just be sure it's something soft. A young woman I know once got so furious that she hit the steering wheel of her car — and broke her arm.

What happens when you start facing your "imperfect" feelings? You also start realizing that maybe, *just maybe,* you're slightly "imperfect" your-self. And that's a positive step toward taking control of your perfectionism — and your life.

It's okay to be imperfect. We live in an imperfect world. Which, as it happens, is lucky for us. Imagine what it would be like to live in a *perfect* world. No problems, no pain, no challenges, no mysteries, no excitement, no creativity, no risks.

BORING

If you want to read more about some of the ideas in this chapter, try:

How To Get Control of Your Time and Your Life by Alan Lakein (New York: New American Library, 1974)

Mindstorms: Children, Computers, and Powerful Ideas by Seymour Papert, Ph.D. (New York: Basic Books, Inc., 1982)

CHAPTER 8

LEARNING TO REWARD YOURSELF AND SAVOR SUCCESS

"Eighth grade was a real turning point in my life," says Daniel, 16. "Up until then my father had worked for a large corporation and was very perfectionist, driven, and competitive. Suddenly he decided to change things. He quit the corporation and started his own business.

"Meanwhile I was on the school swim team. I was perfectionist, driven, and competitive, too — just like my father. One day I hurt my ankle and wasn't able to compete anymore.

"This all happened at around the same time, and it made a BIG change in our family. Everyone loosened up and started doing more things together. Instead of running in different directions, we sat around the dinner table in the evenings and talked. We even took vacations!"

"During my freshman year in college," says Tammy, 20, "my best friend and roommate died in her sleep. It was a terrible shock. Kelly had a congenital heart defect which no one knew about until it was too late.

"I spent a lot of time thinking about Kelly and why she had died and what it all meant. I started realizing how hard it is to plan for tomorrow, since you may not even have a tomorrow. And I started realizing that life is short and precious and you should make the most of it.

"There were things I wanted to do, but I had been putting them off. Now I decided not to wait any longer. I started running a mile a day, then two, then three. I learned how to paint with watercolors. I said 'yes' to dates instead of always staying in my room studying. I started having fun!"

"My mother's stroke really opened my eyes," says Alice, 17. "She's okay now, but for a while it was scary. She was always such a perfectionist and a Type A besides. After the stroke she had to slow down and take it easy. She started going to a behavior modification program for Type A people, and she's a lot different than she used to be.

"Her stroke forced *me* to start looking at my *own* perfectionist tendencies. There are more important things in life than being picky, picky, picky. Now I consciously try to relax more, to not be so hard on myself and other people, and to let things go when I can't change them — or shouldn't bother.

"I used to be proud of being a perfectionist. Now I don't think the stress and pressure are worth it."

The decision to be less perfectionist is a personal and private one. No one can make it for you. It's something you have to choose for yourself. Daniel, Tammy, and Alice all did — but only after going through a "conversion" experience as a result of a major life change. Before then, they were just as perfectionist as you are!

But maybe you don't have to wait for a crisis or a disaster. Maybe you can make an informed, proactive decision instead of a reactive one. From reading this book, you should have a good sense of what perfectionism can do to your mind, your body, your relationships, and your life. Maybe that's all it will take for you to start letting go.

You can choose to change. In Chapter 5, we talked about ways to ease up on yourself. In Chapter 7, we explored ways to take control of your life. These are all positive actions you can take to make your life less driven, less stressful, and more enjoyable. And maybe you're already trying some of them.

In fact, maybe you're hard at work trying to do a perfect job of becoming less perfectionist.

Whoa! Time out! Becoming less perfectionist shouldn't create more ways for you to be hard on yourself, push yourself, and feel bad because you're not doing it all. In fact, an important part of becoming less perfectionist involves feeling good about yourself for who you are. And that involves believing that you *deserve* to feel good about yourself. And when you believe that, you start treating yourself better.

When was the last time you patted yourself on the back, pampered yourself, or let yourself relax and enjoy life? Maybe it's been so long that you've forgotten how.

Let's do something about that.

Low-Cost (or No-Cost) Rewards to Give Yourself

You may need to practice being good to you. Here's a warm-up exercise. You'll need two blank sheets of paper and a pencil or pen.

1. Start by numbering from 1 to 20 down the lefthand side of one sheet of paper. Now list — in the order they occur to you — your major accomplishments. With one restriction: do NOT list any grades, first places, or best ofs.

What's left? How about accomplishments in your personal relationships? Ideas of which you're especially proud? Solutions to problems in your everyday life that you've come up with on your own? Ways in which you've helped people or let them help you? What about your first jump off the high-dive, or the time you mowed your neighbor's lawn, or the day you passed your driver's test? What about the afternoon you made a loaf of bread from scratch and it wasn't just edible, it was delicious?

2. Number from 1 to 20 down the lefthand side of the other sheet of paper. Now list the events in your life that gave you the most pleasure. You can start as far back in time as you like.

Again, no fair including the sixth-grade state spelling bee you won, or the time you took first prize in the gymnastics meet. Instead, what about the wintry Saturday afternoon when your mom taught you how to play monopoly? Or the day your dad took you to a movie without the rest of the family? What about the concert you went to last summer? Or the vacation you took with your best friend's family to the Blue Ridge Mountains?

Interestingly, the events we remember most clearly and fondly are often those that didn't take much time or effort. And they probably didn't have much to do with the things normally devote our energy to pursuing — like getting good grades or beating out the competition.

3.   Finally, put your two lists side-by-side (the better to see them both at once). Choose an item off the first list that you think is worthy of a reward. Then choose something off the second list you'd like to do again as a way of rewarding yourself.

Maybe you can't repeat that vacation — but what about asking your mom for a Monopoly rematch? Or inviting your dad to a movie?

Can you think of brand-new ways to reward yourself? Are there things you've always wanted to do? (Not *accomplish* — just *do*.) Like throw a dinner party for your best friends, or try your hand at photography, or go stargazing at midnight, or listen to "La Boheme?" Make a "wish list" and add to it whenever something else comes to mind.

Because perfectionists are inveterate planners, you may need to build your rewards into your schedule, at least until you form the habit of being good to yourself. If you know that Friday is the big biology test, reserve Friday evening for roller-skating. If your clarinet recital is set for Sunday afternoon, plan to celebrate Sunday evening with your family and friends.

Remember: you deserve it!

Accepting Praise From Others and Praising Yourself

Many perfectionists downplay their accomplishments. Some fall victim to the "impostor syndrome." They seem to sail effortlessly from one achievement to another, but deep down inside they feel like fakes, and they live in constant fear of getting caught. They attribute their success to luck, good timing, or some other factor that's out of their control. They can't accept praise from others because they honestly don't feel they deserve it. They wave it aside or change the subject.

See if any of these confessions sound familiar to you:

"Whenever I aced a math quiz, I always thought it was because I had just happened to study the right homework problems the night before. I was sure that if I had studied other problems I would have failed. It took a long time to admit to myself that I was actually good at math."

Melanie, 14

"My teachers liked me a lot, but I could never really trust them. I was afraid that one day they would see the real me — the unlikeable person I thought I was."

Steven, 12

"When I was made first-chair violin in our school orchestra, I thought it was all over — that the conductor would finally discover I couldn't really play and had been bluffing all along. It wasn't until the next year, when it happened again, that I started thinking that maybe I had talent!"

Alisha, 17

Do you make excuses for your ability? Do you get uncomfortable when people praise you? Does it sometimes seem as though you're hiding behind a facade, a bogus you that only *looks* good?

The next time someone offers you a compliment, try this: Open your mouth and say "thank you." Not "thank you, but . . . " — just "thank you." It will be all over before you know it. It's easier than you think!

When we refuse to accept a compliment, it's like refusing to accept a gift, and that insults the giver. Even if you don't think you deserve to be praised — even if you feel like an impostor — you can still be polite and gracious. After a while, you may start believing your ears. And you may actually start enjoying it when people say wonderful things about you to your face.

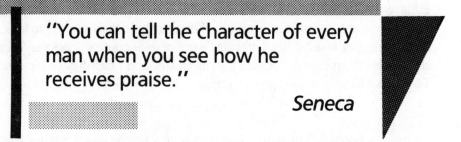

"You can tell the character of every man when you see how he receives praise."

Seneca

You *should* feel terrific when someone says "Good job!" or "You look great today!" or "Congratulations!" We all need the approval of others. And they need our approval, too. If you're the overcritical type (another perfectionist trait), try substituting nice words for "helpful suggestions." Your mom may go into shock the first time you give her a compliment, especially if you haven't done it for years, but you'll both feel better for it.

What about praising yourself? Many perfectionists find this especially hard to do. No matter how well they do something, they're convinced that it's still not good enough. Their standards are so high that they can't possibly meet them.

Try this simple exercise in self-praise. Go to a mirror and say, "I'm okay." It may feel weird at first, but keep doing it until you start believing it. You'll come away with renewed self-confidence and a more positive self-image.

Savoring Your Success

It's your first time ever on skis. You stand there feeling foolish while babies barely out of diapers whiz past on both sides. Your parents are patient, but you wish you were anywhere else.

Deep breath ... bend those knees ... grasp those poles ... take that first hesitant sliding step ... and you're off! An hour later you're unbuckling your skis, red-faced and panting and proud of yourself. You fell down a few times, but you did it!

Or it's your first time ever in front of a large audience. You're the magician in the annual school talent show, and now you're wishing you could make yourself disappear.

Deep breath ... stand up straight ... reach into hat ... and pull out rabbit. Everyone applauds! The rest of the show sails by without a hitch — even the part where you saw your history teacher in half. You're a hit!

Take time — *make* time — to savor your successes. Perfectionists have a habit of doing one thing after another without ever pausing to feel good about what they just accomplished. Put your feet up, relax, and go over the details in your mind. Focus on your triumphs and ignore your mistakes.

Do you have trouble relaxing? That's another common characteristic among perfectionists. They're so busy trying to do everything right that they can't slow down long enough to take it easy.

The inability to relax has become such a problem in our culture that hospitals and clinics offer stress-reduction programs aimed at helping people to loosen up. Before you go that far, here are things you can try at home.

■ **Meditation.**

Go back to "5 Safe Ways to Stay Awake" in Chapter 3 for a description of *very* basic meditation. If you want to know more about this tried-and-true rejuvenator, read about it at the library. Or ask around among your friends or their parents. In the 1960s and 1970s meditation became popular in the United States, and many people tried many different kinds: Zen meditation, transcendental meditation, yoga meditation, and Tai Chi Ch'Uan (which combines slow, graceful physical movements with meditation). It's not at all unlikely that some of your friends' parents tried one or more of these, and they might be able to give you a few pointers.

Meditation works. Galvanic skin response (which is higher when you're relaxed) has been observed to *quadruple* in some meditators. It only *doubles* when you're asleep. Your heartbeat and whole metabolism slows. Your oxygen consumption goes down. And you emerge refreshed and alert.

■ **Listening to soothing music.**

Music to relax by has become increasingly popular in our stressed-out society. Some uses natural sounds (wind blowing through trees, waves rolling in, birds or whales singing); some "new age" music uses electronic synthesizers to generate brand-new sounds. Start with one or more of these; you'll soon make "finds" of your own.

— The **Solitudes** series. Each album contains a full hour of therapeutic sounds — canoe paddles dipping into water, falling rain, crickets on a country night.

— **Musical Massage.** Gentle, listenable instrumentals.

— Individual artists including Kitaro (*Tenku*), Paul Winter (*Sun Singer, Canyon*), George Winston (*December, Autumn*), and Andreas Vollenweider (*Down to the Moon, White Winds*).

"I think trying to do so many things at one time, or maintaining such a high level of performance for a long time, is really a lot for someone to handle, gifted or otherwise."

Tim, 14

■ **Yoga.**

By breathing, stretching, and moving *slowly* into time-honored positions, you can not only calm down but get into shape. (Raquel Welch has been a practitioner for years.) You may find a class at your local community college or Y. Or go to your bookstore and pick up a copy of *Integral Yoga Hatha* by Yogiraj Sri Swami Satchidananda (New York: Holt, Rinehart and Winston, 1970), a clear introduction to basic yoga techniques, with lots of illustrations.

■ **Cooking.**

Fix a pan of fudge . . . chop a pound of veggies and make homemade soup . . . knead bread . . . fill the kitchen with delicious smells. Many people claim that cooking relaxes them. There's something about the simple chores of peeling potatoes, measuring flour, and stirring a pan on the stove that gets your mind off your troubles.

■ **Walking.**

Stroll around the block, or ask a favorite friend to accompany you through a park or nature reserve. Go at a leisurely pace, giving yourself a chance to notice the things around you — the smells of the woods, the sounds of children playing in a park, the colors of new or changing leaves.

Yes, relaxing takes time, but it's time well spent. You think more clearly, your body works better, and you have more energy. Try to make it part of your daily routine and you'll immediately feel the difference.

> "If a man insisted always on being serious, and never allowed himself a bit of fun and relaxation, he would go mad or become unstable without knowing it."
>
> *Herodotus*

Reading for Pleasure

What a luxury it is to read what *you* want to read, instead of plowing through assignments. Many perfectionists don't leave time for this all-important pursuit. Remember how it felt when you were a child and sat up in bed reading, or curled up on a blanket under a tree, or hid in a closet with a flashlight? Those days don't have to be over.

Aren't you about due to reread *The Lord of the Rings?* Or maybe you miss Madeline L'Engle and her *Wrinkle in Time* series. Or maybe you've been meaning to read *Anna Karenina* or *David Copperfield* or *The Decline and Fall of the Roman Empire* or Sandburg's biography of Lincoln or that new collection of short stories you've been eyeing at your local bookstore or . . . .

Reading can be your reward and your relaxation all in one. Most gifted kids are avid readers, so it's no secret to you what pleasures books hold. And no matter how much you read, there's always something you haven't read, waiting like buried treasure to be discovered.

> "Reading is to the mind what exercise is to the body."
> *Sir Richard Steele*

If you won't let yourself do pure leisure reading, how about bibliotherapy? In bibliotherapy, you read books to help you work through a particular problem. If perfectionism is a problem in your life, you may want to try one or more of the books described below. Don't worry if some of them seem too young for you; all that means is they'll take less time to read (and probably have pictures, which *always* make books more interesting).

- *Dreams and Drummers* by Doris Buchanan Smith (New York: Thomas Y. Crowell, 1978). Stephanie is a perfectionist. She has won the blue ribbon in the science fair for the past several years, she has a straight-A average, and she's the first-chair drummer in the band. Plus (to rub it in) she's the prettiest girl in her school. In *Dreams and Drummers,* Stephanie learns what it's like to finish second.

- *Be a Perfect Person in Just Three Days!* by Stephen Manes (Boston: Houghton-Mifflin, 1982). Milo, who wants to be perfect, finds a book by Dr. K. Pinkerton Silverfish that promises to teach him how. He follows all of its instructions to the letter — right down to wearing a broccoli necklace. Read the book and find out why!

■ *The World's Greatest Expert on Absolutely Everything is Crying* by Barbara Botner (New York: Dell, 1986). Katherine Ann is an expert on countless things. She has traveled the world and is a real know-it-all. Then she and her family move to a small town, and suddenly what she wants more than anything is to be accepted by the kids in her new school. It's a revealing look at how perfectionism affects relationships.

"I have sometimes dreamt, at least, that when the Day of Judgment dawns and the great conquerors and lawyers and statesmen come to receive their rewards — their crowns, their laurels, their names carved indelibly upon imperishable marble — the Almighty will turn to Peter and will say, not without a certain envy when he sees us coming with our books under our arms, 'Look, these need no reward. We have nothing to give them here. They have loved reading.'"
Virginia Woolf, The Second Common Reader

Perfectionists may be good at a lot of things, but they're usually *not* very good at rewarding themselves and savoring their success. In the midst of trying to be the best, they forget to enjoy just being themselves.

How can you tell when it's time to cut back on your schedule, relax, and take it easy for a while? One young woman I interviewed offered these wise words: "It's time to slow down when you get so obsessed that you forget the people in your life, your faith, and your hobbies."

CHAPTER 9

HOW TO GET OTHERS TO EASE UP ON YOU

If your parents are human, they've probably said, "We only want what's best for you." The trouble is, what they often mean is "We only want you to *be* the best." There's a GIGANTIC difference, but even the smartest, nicest, most with-it parents can't see it sometimes.

What they think of as loving encouragement turns into pressure. "We know you can do a good job on that test" becomes "We expect you to get an A." Or "Try your hardest to win the race" becomes "We know you can come in first." Or "We think you should go to college" becomes "We want you to apply to Yale and Harvard and Stanford and get a law degree and go to work in your Uncle Fred's firm."

I know a woman who used to cry whenever her daughter didn't win an essay contest. And her daughter would think, "I have to win or my mother will cry and it will be all my fault." Another woman used to actually spank her daughter when she didn't win a baton-twirling competition. Naturally the daughter grew to hate baton and eventually quit it; she seldom performed well because she was terrified of what would happen if she didn't.

One father, angered because his son didn't take first place in a piano competition, stormed up to a judge and said, "I want to know what else my son can go into since he didn't win the prize today." The judge replied, "He can go into a library and read a book, or he can go into your yard and mow the lawn, or he can go into his room and draw a picture." The father walked away angry, but what the judge said was right on: The boy had many options, and his life wasn't over just because he hadn't won that particular competition on that particular day.

PARENTS SAY THE DUMBEST THINGS

"When I make a mistake or don't do something right the first time, my mom always says, 'What's wrong with you? I thought you were supposed to be gifted.'"
— Nathan, 15

"My mother checks my homework nightly and when she finds a mistake she says, 'See, you're not so smart!'"
— Talia, 13

"My father always introduces me as 'My Son, The Brain.'"
— Sam, 12

"Whenever I get straight A's, my parents act like it's no big deal. But when I get a B it's always 'What happened here? Don't you pay attention in class? What's wrong with you?'"
— Courtney, 16

"My father redid my whole science project. When I told him I was supposed to do it myself, he said, 'I'm just making you look better.'"
— David, 15

While I was writing my dissertation, I asked several college students to take the Perfectionism Scale, a test for perfectionism developed by Dr. David Burns, a psychiatrist at the Presbyterian-University of Pennsylvania Medical Center. Afterward I interviewed the ten highest scorers (those who tested most perfectionist) and the ten lowest scorers (those who tested least perfectionist). I asked them to tell me the kinds of things their parents used to tell them when they were kids.

The differences were fascinating — and revealing. The ten most perfectionist students had grown up hearing things like "A job worth doing is worth doing well" . . . "Always finish what you start" . . . "Be number one" . . . "You can be class valedictorian someday" . . . "We want you to get all A's" . . . "If you get any grade but an A, make sure it's an A + ." The ten least perfectionist students had grown up hearing things like "Just do the best you can" . . . "You win some, you lose some" . . . "Better luck next time" . . . "What's done is done" . . . "Live for today and don't worry about tomorrow."

The parents of the most perfectionist students had always had overly high expectations of them. The parents of the least perfectionist students had been more relaxed and accepting.

Some parents try to relive their own lives through their children's accomplishments. They see their children as a second chance to do all the things they never got around to. They sign them up for piano lessons because *they* always wanted to study piano, or they insist that their kids apply to certain colleges because *they* always wanted to go there.

Similarly, parents don't want their children to make the same mistakes they made when they were younger. On the surface, there's nothing wrong with that. It's natural to want to protect someone you love from getting hurt. The trouble is that mistakes often lead the way toward learning. Parents who protect their children too much are depriving them of the opportunity to learn from their mistakes.

What can you do if your parents are a pain? You can mount an Anti-Perfectionism Campaign around your house. Like any effective campaign, this one will take planning and persistence.

How to Run an Anti-Perfectionism Campaign

Start by letting your parents know how you feel.

"You must be crazy," one young woman said when I suggested that she try this. "They'll hit the roof if I tell them to ease up on me. They'll think I'm just making excuses for not being first and best in everything I do."

RULE #1
NEVER UNDERESTIMATE YOUR PARENTS

They may seem dense, but they're not stupid. And they really *do* care about you. And because they care about you, they'll probably be willing to listen if you approach them semi-politely and say, "Mom, Dad, we have a problem and we need to talk."

Many parents honestly don't realize that perfectionism can be harmful. They think that all the late nights and stress are normal, natural, and necessary parts of making the grade. Remember that there's a good chance your parents are perfectionists, too. If their own lifestyle is crazy and pressured, they probably think that everyone who wants to succeed has to live that way.

Here's your chance to teach *them* something. You can start by trying to share this book with them. Tell them how perfectionism is affecting your mind, your body, and your relationships. (Be prepared with a few juicy examples.)

CAUTION

Your parents may not be willing to read this book, discuss perfectionism with you, or do anything else suggested in this chapter. They may resent any efforts you make to communicate with them about perfectionism. They may refuse to reconsider their own perfectionist tendencies, their too-high expectations of you, or the need to change their behavior toward you in any way.

This doesn't mean that you can't continue to help yourself. It doesn't mean that you can't keep working on your own perfectionist tendencies. It doesn't mean that you can't talk to other adults — teachers, counselors, pastors or priests or rabbis. It just means that you'll have to continue on your own. But you already do a lot of things independently; why not this, too?

If your parents seem interested and receptive, go on to suggest that all of you do Dr. Burns's Perfectionism Scale exercise. You'll find it here, complete with instructions. You go first, followed by each of your parents in turn. Afterward, compare your scores.

THE PERFECTIONISM SCALE*

Read each statement, then rate each one according to whether you *strongly agree* (+ 2), *agree somewhat* (+ 1), *can't decide* (0), *disagree somewhat* (-1), or *strongly disagree* (-2.) Answer with your *first thought* to get the truest response.

———— 1. If I don't set the highest standards for myself, I am likely to end up a second-rate person.

* Permission to reprint the Perfectionism Scale is granted by the author, David D. Burns, M.D.

_____ 2. People will probably think less of me if I make a mistake.

_____ 3. If I cannot do something really well, there is little point in doing it at all.

_____ 4. I should be upset if I make a mistake.

_____ 5. If I try hard enough, I should be able to excel at anything I attempt.

_____ 6. It is shameful for me to display weaknesses or foolish behavior.

_____ 7. I shouldn't have to repeat the same mistake many times.

_____ 8. An average performance is bound to be unsatisfying to me.

_____ 9. Failing at something important means I'm less of a person.

_____ 10. If I scold myself for failing to live up to my expectations, it would help me to do better in the future.

Now add up the numbers of your responses to get your total score. To find out what it means, see page to come.

INTERPRETING YOUR SCORE ON THE PERFECTIONISM SCALE

A score of + 20 indicates a high degree of perfectionism; a score of - 20 indicates a low degree of perfectionism. Other scores should be evaluated according to how close they come to the extremes.

Studies suggest that about half of the general population is likely to score between + 2 and + 16.

If you and/or your parents, teachers, grandparents, neighbors, or friends want to know more about perfectionism, the following books are good sources of additional information:

■ *Understanding Success and Failure* by Lois Roets, Ed.D. (New Sharon, IA: Leadership Publishers, 1985). Dr. Roets covers the positive aspects of failures — including what we can learn from them. Of special interest are examples of famous people who experienced failures on their way to success.

■ *Feeling Good: The New Mood Therapy* by David D. Burns, M.D. (New York: New American Library, 1981). See especially Chapter 14.

The more your parents know about perfectionism, the more willing they'll be to field suggestions on how they can ease up on you. Making those suggestions is the next part of your anti-perfectionism campaign.

RULE #2
BE READY TO COMPROMISE

Easing up on you is not the same as letting you have your own way in everything. Don't expect your parents to relax all of their expectations of you. (Think about it: Would you really want them to?) Instead, work together if possible to discover which ones are negotiable.

For example: Your parents have been planning your class schedule for years and telling you which courses to take. But there are some *you* want to take just for fun or because they interest you. Ask your parents to help you decide on the best time to fit them in. If possible, get your school guidance counselor involved in this process.

Or: You've been delivering straight A's pretty steadily — at the expense of your social life. Your parents probably aren't about to let you leave the house every night of the week, but what about one night, or two?

Try to find other areas where you can all practice some give-and-take. The point is to arrive at a happy medium between their goals for you and your goals for yourself.

RULE #3:
STAY CALM

Any conversation you have with your parents will go a lot more smoothly if you can keep your temper. Maybe you're angry at them for criticizing the B you got in biology, and maybe you have a right to be angry. But instead of stomping and screaming and slamming doors, try simply telling them how you feel. Let them know that you need their love and support. Chances are you'll get it.

If you really *can't* talk to your parents, how about writing them a letter? (Even an *anonymous* letter?) Or if you choose to do a school paper on perfectionism or procrastination, let them read it. When I finished writing my dissertation, I gave a copy to my mother. That provided the basis for one of the best conversations we've ever had.

Making Your Campaign Public

Once you've got your parents on your side, it becomes easier to face the rest of the world — including the teachers, friends, and peers who are always putting the pressure on you to be perfect.

"Living up to being labeled gifted can be a problem in school. I wish teachers would realize that just because you're gifted doesn't mean you're smart in every subject."

Charles, 14

"My geometry teacher knows I get straight A's in all my other courses. He's always saying things like, 'I know you can do better in this class. I don't think you're trying hard enough.'"

Kimberley, 15

For many kids, the problem starts with an older brother or sister who seems to do everything right. You know the story: A younger sibling walks into a class and teacher says, "You're Alex Pinkerton? I knew your brother Mike; he was the best student I ever had." Who can live up to that? Who even wants to try?

Like parents, teachers have expectations. Like parents, they sometimes say dumb things. Like parents, they're worth talking to. Give it a try. It's okay to say, "Ms. Murkle, I wish you wouldn't compare me to my sister."

If your friends hang around with you just because you're a straight-A student or president of your class or captain of the football team, maybe you should make new friends. Suzie, 16, remembers the first (and last) time she went out with a boy from her philosophy class. She enjoyed herself right up to the moment he walked her to her door and asked to borrow her philosophy notes.

Peers may have mixed feelings about bright, super-achieving classmates. They may admire them on the one hand and be extremely jealous on the other. They may send mixed messages that are difficult to decipher.

"The other kids in my class put me down for being smart. They call me 'Einstein' and act shocked if I get a grade lower than an A."
Jason, 14

"My best friend and I are at the top of our class. We like each other a lot, but it seems like we're always competing with each other."
Erin, 13

"My friends resent me for being smart. Sometimes I deliberately answer test questions wrong so I'll get a lower grade and they'll accept me more."
Timothy, 15

If some of your friends are also perfectionists, consider forming a support group. Start with a few ground rules, including *no competition allowed.* Use this group as a place to laugh at your mistakes, talk about your problems with perfectionism, share your procrastination stories, and encourage one another in the healthy pursuit of excellence.

Duke University in Durham, North Carolina offers group counseling for perfectionists. Students in the groups sessions make up sayings or slogans which reinforce anti-perfectionism and design anti-perfectionism posters to display on walls. They share "war stories" about their own push for perfection — and realize once and for all that they're not alone. They give one another support. They use humor and laughter to relieve the stress they're under. The work together to transform their perfectionism into a healthy pursuit of excellence.

Finally, if you have a part-time job, you may need to take your anti-perfectionism campaign there as well. Some businesses make hiring decisions on the basis of student grades. They assume — often correctly — that high-achieving students will be high-performing, responsible workers. You can *do* your best without having to *be* the best. And you should be allowed to make mistakes.

Although few student jobs involve the kinds of risk-taking and decision-making adults confront in their careers, it's still interesting to know the results of a study Dr. David Burns did with insurance salespeople. He found that the perfectionists made an average of $15,000 per year *less* than the non-perfectionists. The perfectionists were painstaking and very detail-oriented, but they lacked something the non-perfectionists seemed to have plenty of: the willingness to take chances, to grow and to learn.

"The closest to perfection a person ever comes is when he fills out a job application form."
Stanley Randall

CHAPTER 10

WHEN AND HOW TO GET HELP COPING

When the French historian Alexis de Tocqueville visited the United States in 1835, he observed that Americans "all have a lively faith in the perfectability of man." More than 150 years later, it's still true. As a culture we're eternally in search of the perfect mate, the perfect job, the perfect body, the perfect family. No wonder your parents keep hoping for you to be the perfect child. No wonder you keep trying to be that perfect child — and perfect student, perfect friend, perfect, etc.

The fact is, there's simply no way to achieve earthly perfection.

In 1841 a man named John Humphrey Noyes established a religious community called the Perfectionists. Six years later, in 1847, they formed a colony in Oneida, New York. Noyes taught that anyone who converted to Perfectionism would be free from sin. The people in his community even tried breeding human beings to get perfect children. In 1879 the colony was abandoned — because it was "imperfect." Today all that's left of Noyes's plan is the Oneida company, which manufactures silverplate and stainless-steel flatware. It's nice, but it's not perfect.

Countless other religious groups have tried for perfection and failed. Philosophers, artists, and scientists have tried it and failed. Adolf Hitler and the Third Reich tried it and failed.

It never works. It can't work. Forget it! Instead, focus on being yourself, on being human. That's a big enough job all by itself.

> "When a man says that he is perfect . . . there is only one of two places for him, and that is heaven or the lunatic asylum."
> *Henry Ward Beecher*

If you need help coping, it's available. All you have to do is ask. Talk to your parents, your school counselor, or your minister, priest, or rabbi. Talk to your teachers. Talk to your friends. Form around you a group of people who will hear you out, give you good advice, support you, and appreciate you for who you are, not who they think you should be.

If you think you need professional help, there are counselors who specialize in working with perfectionists. Many communities have mental health centers, some with walk-in counseling. It takes brains to realize when you can't go it alone. The smart people are the ones who admit it and do something about it. The not-so-smart people are the ones who hold it inside, keep it a secret, go it alone — and get deeper into trouble.

How to Tell When It's Time to Get Help

If you have perfectionist tendencies, chances are you'll always have them. Problems arise when you carry them too far.

How can you tell when you've crossed that line? Think back to the differences between perfectionism and the healthy pursuit of excellence described in the introduction to this book. (Or go back and reread them to refresh your memory.) Understanding these differences is key to knowing which side of the line you're on.

Generally speaking, pursuers of excellence enjoy the things they do. When they finish a project, they pat themselves on the back and reward themselves. They take honest pride in their work and learn from their mistakes. They're committed but not obsessive, dedicated but not desperate. They know how to relax and have a good time.

Perfectionists, on the other hand, always aim higher than they can reach. They don't know how to enjoy their work or take pride in their accomplishments. When they finish a project, they torture themselves with *if onlys* and *shoulds.* "If only I had done it this way" . . . "I should have taken more time" . . . "If only I had done one more thing" . . . "I should have done something else." They stay trapped in the "failure gap" between what is and what might have been.

Perfectionists are never satisfied with living in the present. They're always looking back with regret or forward with apprehension and fear. For them, the future holds the promise of gloom and doom. "I wonder what terrible thing will happen to me next" . . . "What else can go wrong in my life?" . . . "Why am I so unlucky?" They feel as if fate has given them a bad hand of cards and may perceive other people (and the world in general) as out to get them.

One way to distinguish between the pursuit of excellence and perfectionism is by the kind of self-talk you use. Pursuers of excellence use positive self-talk: "Hey, I did a pretty good job," "I'm really proud of myself," "I enjoyed working on that project," "Maybe I didn't take first place, but I tried my hardest, and I feel good about that." Perfectionists use negative self-talk: "Why can't I ever do anything right?," "Look at those two questions I missed," "I just know I'm going to fail," "People are going to figure out that I'm a fake."

While a little bit of negative self-talk is okay, a lot is not. If you're always hard on yourself, you need to find out why. Is it an old, bad habit? Or has something happened recently to make you feel more than usually down and depressed? If you can't sort it out yourself, get help. Go to your parents, a teacher, your school counselor, your minister or priest or rabbi.

Pursuers of excellence can experience periods of perfectionism — times when the going is especially rough, or they have a major setback or failure and slip into negative thought patterns. These periods are no cause for alarm, unless they last longer than a day or two. If you feel as if you've fallen into an emotional hole you can't climb out of, get help. **If you need help right away,** turn to page 112 and call one of the numbers listed there.

Perfectionism and Teenage Suicide

The teenage suicide rate has risen dramatically in recent years. Since 1955 it has climbed more than 300 percent; between 1960 and 1980 alone it rose by an alarming 136 percent. According to the National Committee on Youth Suicide Prevention, it's the third leading killer of young people in the United States between ages 15 and 24. They estimate that over half a million teens attempt suicide every year — and over 6,000 succeed.

These statistics may be too low. Suicides are often classified as homicides to spare the family grief and avoid the stigma they place on a community. Some people believe that the actual number may be four times as great: *two million* attempts each year and nearly *25,000* deaths.

In 1986 John Kinkel, Ph.D., assistant professor of sociology at the University of Michigan at Flint, presented a report to the American Psychiatric Association claiming that nearly eight out of every hundred teens in America attempted suicide in 1985. The United States House of Representatives recently allocated $1 million for schools and nonprofit agencies to use for youth suicide prevention programs.

Why do kids kill themselves? One reason may be perfectionism. This is not to say that *all* teenage suicides are related to perfectionism — but it's almost certain that some of them are.

It takes courage to live. It takes courage to be human. It takes courage to make mistakes, and it takes courage to admit them and even laugh at them. *It takes courage to be imperfect.* Especially in a culture as competitive as ours.

Suicide isn't unique to any one race, class, or IQ level. But people with above-average intelligence seem more prone to it than others. Plus they may also have these characteristics as well:

1. They have extremely high expectations of themselves and/or other people.

2. They form extremely intense relationships.

3. They have a hard time accepting the fact that failure and loss are normal parts of living and being human.

Which group is most likely to have all of these traits? Gifted teens — particularly gifted *perfectionist* teens.

TWENTY-TWO SIGNS
OF A TEEN IN TROUBLE

Experts have found that teens at risk for becoming suicidal show danger signs in advance. *If you notice any of these signs in yourself, talk to somebody. If you notice any of them in a friend, tell somebody.*

- [ ] Sudden changes in personality
- [ ] Sudden changes in eating or sleeping habits
- [ ] Sudden changes in behavior
- [ ] Drug and/or alcohol abuse
- [ ] Lack of interest in or withdrawal from planned activities (sports, clubs, social events, etc.)
- [ ] Persistent boredom
- [ ] Severe depression that lasts a week or longer
- [ ] Withdrawal from family and friends; self-imposed isolation
- [ ] Inability to have fun
- [ ] Concealed or direct suicide threats
- [ ] Loss of interest in personal grooming
- [ ] Psychosomatic illness (meaning an illness with no apparent physical cause)
- [ ] Preoccupation with death and death-related themes
- [ ] Giving away prized possessions to family and friends
- [ ] Saying goodbye to family and friends
- [ ] Difficulty concentrating
- [ ] An unexplained decline in the quality of schoolwork
- [ ] A recent suicide of a friend or relative
- [ ] A previous suicide attempt
- [ ] Talking about suicide, either jokingly or seriously
- [ ] Running away from home, family, school, etc.
- [ ] Feelings of meaninglessness in life

Remember that *you always have options.* You can correct mistakes. You can change your mind. You can switch directions from a dead-end road to a positive alternate path. You can rack up failures and still be a success. (Like the "Ten Famous People Who Blew It" from Chapter 5.) The only time you *don't* have options is if you're not around to exercise them.

No problem is so overwhelming that suicide is the only solution. If you feel you need more information about suicide right away, you can contact any of the following:

■ Look under **SUICIDE PREVENTION** in your local phone book. Most cities and many towns have suicide prevention hotlines, staffed 24 hours a day with people ready and willing to listen.

■ **Metro-Help** Phone: 1-800-621-4000
This is a toll-free, 24-hour, seven days a week, national crisis hotline for suicidal and runaway youths.

■ **American Association of Suicidology** 2459 South Ash St., Denver, CO 80222   Phone: (303) 692-0985
This national clearinghouse is open during business hours (Monday-Friday, 9-5) and can refer you to the crisis center nearest you.

■ **The National Committee on Youth Suicide Prevention** 67 Irving Place So., New York, NY 10003   Phone: (212) 677-6666
This organization can provide information and articles on youth suicide and prevention. It has established suicide prevention committees in most states and can refer you to the one nearest you.

■ **Youth Suicide National Center** 1825 I St. N.W., Suite 400, Washington, D.C. 20006   Phone: (202) 429-2016
This organization sends representatives to schools, conducts youth-oriented programs on suicide prevention, provides counseling, and mails out information on suicide.

Many schools, concerned with the rising teen suicide rate, are bringing this sensitive topic into their curriculum. You may want to talk to a teacher about the possibility of a special class or discussion session.

Finally: Suicidal thoughts cross almost everyone's mind from time to time. It's not unusual to "flash" on it when you're in the depths of depression or despair.

Even people who seem to have it all — fame, money, and success — have considered suicide. When Billy Joel found himself thinking about it, he wrote the song "You're Only Human," made a record, and donated the money from the sales to the National Center on Youth Suicide Prevention.

YOU'RE ONLY HUMAN (SECOND WIND)

You're having a hard time and lately you don't feel so good
You're getting a bad reputation in your neighborhood
It's alright, it's alright
Sometimes that's what it takes
You're only human, you're allowed to make your share of mistakes

You better believe there will be times in your life
When you'll be feeling like a stumbling fool
So take it from me you'll learn more from your accidents
Than anything that you could ever learn at school

Don't forget your second wind
Sooner or later you'll get your second wind
It's not always easy to be living in this world of pain
You're gonna be crashing into stone walls again and again
It's alright, it's alright
Though you feel your heart break
You're only human, you're gonna have to deal with heartache
Just like a boxer in a title fight
You got to walk in that ring all alone
You're not the only one who's made mistakes
But they're the only things you can truly call your own
Don't forget your second wind
Wait in your corner until that breeze blows in

You've been keeping to yourself these days
Cause you're thinking everything's gone wrong
Sometimes you just want to lay down and die
That emotion can be so strong
But hold on
Till that old second wind comes along

You probably don't want to hear advice from someone else
But I wouldn't be telling you if I hadn't been there myself
It's alright, it's alright
Sometimes that's all it takes
We're only human
We're supposed to make mistakes
But I survived all those long lonely days
When it seemed I did not have a friend
Cause all I needed was a little faith
So I could catch my breath and face the world again
Don't forget your second wind
Sooner or later you'll feel that momentum kick in
Don't forget your second wind
Sooner or later you'll feel that momentum kick in

> "To affirm life is to deepen, to make more inward, and to exalt the will to live."
> *Albert Schweitzer*

Failure + Flexibility = Fantastic!

If you have read this book all the way through from the first page to these words, then you already know how normal it is to fail and how necessary it is to be flexible — in setting your goals, in adapting to change, in planning alternate paths.

It's the *combination* of these two — failure and flexibility — that seems to yield the most fantastic results where human achievement is concerned.

The Ten Famous People Who Blew It failed, flopped, flunked and goofed many times during their lives. But they turned their failures into successes. (Practice may not make perfect, but enough of it — even practice at failing! — makes possibilities.)

A new business school, The Institute for the Study of Free Enterprise, was recently started at the University of North Carolina at Chapel Hill. The teachers are all successful businessmen and women. Interestingly, one of the requirements for getting a teaching position there is a *history of failures*. The Institute isn't interested in people who have never known failure. They simply don't have the learning and experience with being flexible that the new school believes its students need.

Successful people are those who can blow it and bounce back. They don't sit there feeling sorry for themselves. They get up, dust themselves off, and head in another direction — and keep doing it until they end up where they want to go.

If you could look back at your life and remember every minute, you'd find many failures you've since forgotten. And some of them would surprise you.

What happened the first time you tried to walk? You fell down. The first time you tried to ride a bike? You ran into a tree or skidded off a curve. The first time you tried to hit a baseball with a bat? It whizzed by your nose and you swung at the air. The first time you tried to swim? You splashed and sloshed like a sorry fish.

In fact, *any* life is a series of failures, an assortment of mistakes, a collection of blunders and missteps. If you've been worrying about failure — stop. Instead, think about what you'd be missing if you never took chances, never took risks, never took that first step toward an uncertain conclusion. Think about what life would be like if you really *were* perfect. Then be glad you're not!

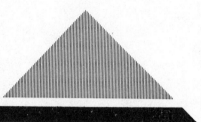

"We ought to dance with rapture that we should be alive and in the flesh, and part of the living, incarnate cosmos. I am part of the sun as my eye is part of me. That I am part of the earth my feet know perfectly, and my blood is part of the sea. My soul knows that I am part of the human race . . . . "

D.H. Lawrence

If you want to read more about some of the ideas in this chapter, try:

Pathfinders by Gail Sheehy (New York: Bantam Books, 1982)

When Living Hurts by Sol Gordon (New York: Union of American Hebrew Congregations, 1985)

INDEX